*Holiness Is Wholeness
and Other Essays*

Holiness Is Wholeness
and Other Essays

JOSEF GOLDBRUNNER

UNIVERSITY OF NOTRE DAME PRESS • 1964

The translation of Heiligkeit und Gesundheit (Holiness Is Wholeness) *(Herder Verlag, Frieburg) was made by Stanley Godman for the English edition published in 1955 by Burns, Oates, and Washbourne, Ltd., London. The essay has also been translated into French, Spanish, Portuguese and Italian.*

The translation of the additional essays contained in this new American edition was supervised by the University of Notre Dame Press.

Imprimi Potest: Howard J. Kenna, C.S.C.,
    Provincial

Nihil Obstat: Joseph Hoffman, C.S.C.,
    Censor Deputatus

Imprimatur: ✠ Leo A. Pursley, D.D.,
    Bishop of Fort Wayne-South Bend

Second Printing   1965
Third Printing Sept., 1965

Copyright 1964 by

The University of Notre Dame Press
Notre Dame, Indiana

Library of Congress Catalog Card Number: 64-23667

Manufactured in the United States of America

CONTENTS

1   1

HOLINESS IS WHOLENESS

2   35

PSYCHOTHERAPY AND PASTORAL CARE

3   46

PASTORAL CARE CALLS THE PERSON

4   60

CHARACTERISTICS OF RELIGIOUS LIFE TODAY

5   73

PSYCHOTHERAPY AND CONFESSION

6   85

PASTORAL CARE FOR SCRUPLES

PREFACE

At the request of many listeners these lectures are being published for the benefit of a wider public. The purpose is to draw the attention of priests and educators to a new field of human knowledge, namely depth-psychology. Hardly a book on the work of the priest appears nowadays which does not contain a contribution to this subject. The intention of this present book is, however, not only to demonstrate the significance of modern psychology for the spiritual adviser, by giving help for the treatment of the spiritually sick, that is, by serving the needs of the specialist in this branch of the cure of souls. Its concern is rather to show by examples how the new knowledge of the soul can be fruitfully used in the promotion of spiritual health and may prepare the way for the religious life.

1: HOLINESS IS WHOLENESS

CONDITIONS FOR A HEALTHY SPIRITUAL LIFE

Three Theses

God, the All-Holy, is freely-flowing and flourishing Life. He is whole; there is no blemish of disease in Him, no poison of death. In Him lies our health and salvation; in His nearness is healing for body and soul. The striving after the Godlike makes for health and wholeness. The more we seek the perfection that makes man like God, that makes him holy, the more we should become healthy in body and soul, for holiness is health.

But between us and God stands death. The approach to God, the all-holy, exposes man to the influence of death and to the poison of death which causes disease. Thus the statement "Holiness is health" appears to be opposed by a counterstatement: "The striving after holiness produces a crisis in the body and makes for ill health." Such is the experience of the mystics. Tauler expresses it in an image. When a man, he says, goes out to seek God and tries to catch Him as though with a net, the net, which is his bodily nature, will inevitably break—as with the miraculous haul of fishes, when the net could no longer hold the overwhelming abundance of the catch. "When a man," says Tauler, "achieves such a catch, nature, which is too weak to hold it, must break, and the man will never again have a day's good health." And

St. Hildegard writes: "God rarely dwells in a healthy body." These diseases of the body do not come from outside but from the overflowing of the Godhead, which has so flooded a man's soul that the poor earthly body can contain it no longer. It is the experience of the mystics that the nearness of God is fatal to the body. "No man shall see Me and remain alive." Such is the profound implication of the Christian message that the way to God is the way of the cross, at the end of which a slow death must be endured until all human transitoriness is no more. Only in death can man be transformed into the likeness of God.

It is a law of the quest for perfection that the way to holiness leads through death. Only as man follows Christ in the way of the cross does he become like God. Fear of the cross has tended to obscure this law in the doctrine of the Christian life. We have a premonition of the way it operates in the peculiar physical exhaustion we feel—after a religious service, perhaps—which has brought us close to the realities of God, after a lesson on the scriptures which has given us a taste of the word of God, or after a sermon, when the preacher has been wholly the instrument of the gospel. Spiritual life is a strain on our health. An excess of it can turn this physical exhaustion into a crisis affecting the whole body. Only a slow advance in the spiritual life gives the body time to adapt itself, to expel, as it were, the poison of death which it has come to absorb. When this happens, a higher level of health occurs. One can see it, sometimes, in the case of old monks, whose bodies are radiant with a tender, transparent, spiritualized health. Grace, in such a case, enhances nature. But with many saints we hear of physical collapse in the course of their development. I would call these illnesses "legitimate maladies" in the striving after holiness. They follow from the original sin in which man stands before God. They are a transition on the way to holiness; they belong to the way of the cross, which Christ trod before us and calls us to tread: "It is the man who loses his life for my sake and for the gospel's sake, that will save it" (Mark 8:35).

In contrast to these legitimate imperilings of bodily health there are other "illegitimate imperilings" of health caused by a striving after holiness. There are unhealthy features in the faces of the saints which are not the expression of true human suffering. We read of illnesses which are not necessary, illnesses of the body and the soul which represent untruth, since they are caused by false attitudes, by false ways of life, by a false conduct of life, not in accordance with the laws of nature nor with the true relationship between the natural and the supernatural. These "illegitimate illnesses" are contrary to nature. But such mutilations of life, physical and spiritual, have become so identified with the very notion of holiness that one almost has to smile, when calling a man a saint, as if to apologize for his manifest oddity.

Modern man is scandalized by the unnaturalness that he seems to see in the faces of some of the saints. Our whole view of man and his nature lies behind this feeling of revulsion. The modern Christian has become sensitive to the natural and the unnatural. He is certainly ready to tread the way of the cross that leads to holiness, but he rebels when holiness appears in a guise contrary to nature. He wants to expose himself to the scorching and transforming sun of God's holiness with his whole body and soul, to stake his whole life on the way of the cross—but not to exclude his natural human body from redemption.

Our knowledge of human nature has made great progress and undergone great changes as a result of modern advances in medicine and psychotherapy. The sick body and the sick soul have taught us the conditions necessary for the healthy body and the healthy soul. This development in the knowledge of man is having an effect on the theory of the Christian life in its striving after holiness and in the realm of asceticism. First of all, we propose to set the body and its health against the striving after holiness, and see the effect of modern ideas of health on Christian asceticism; afterwards an attempt will be made to show the effects of modern psychotherapy on the striving after holiness in life.

The Body in the Striving for Holiness

The sun of radiant holiness appeared in Christ. The early Christians were overwhelmed with a yearning for the Godlike life. The strivings of the spirit tugged impatiently at the chains which hamper and bind it to the earth. From the first violent eruption of the monastic movement, through the Middle Ages to our own time, the tension between body and spirit remains a constant theme. Spiritualization is the aim of all religious striving. War is declared on the body. The dualism is present in all degrees from open hostility to latent suspicion. Asceticism is a constant wrestling with the body, a suppression of all the dangerous forces of nature, a fight against everything that pertains to the senses. Attack is the best form of defense and so the instinctive lower life of the body was resisted with flagellations, fastings and night watches, for the purpose of making it serviceable and tractable.

In his essay on *Health and Holiness* Francis Thompson pillories the "tyranny of the spirit over the body." In his incisive language he calls the "blind tyranny of the spirit against all flesh" a "murderous struggle." "To drive a donkey to death was regarded as cruel, but to do the same to one's own body was thought to be meritorious. The whole apparatus of corporal punishment and castigation was a brutal system for a brutal age," in which men "had a nervous strength bordering on heartlessness." Our ancestors' lives were indefatigably strenuous; they lashed themselves with thongs and wore shirts lined with hair and stiff with their own blood, the mere sight of which struck horror in the beholder. Such an abuse of the body would condemn us today to permanent torpor and debility. Hermits exposed themselves to all the terrors of an inclement climate without succumbing to rheumatism. For constitutions like theirs a strict asceticism was a wholesome antidote; for us it would be merely a useless attempt to deaden our appetites (would that we had appetites to deaden!), to weaken the pining ·flesh, and still further to exhaust a body which our voluptuously-living forefathers have left us too exhausted already. What we need are spurs to force us into life, not a bridle to curb an exuberant *joie de vivre*. Without generalizing unduly, we must agree with Thompson that "the ways and means to holiness seem to have changed because we ourselves have become so different." The suspicion has gradually dawned on us that much of what was formerly blamed on the body should rather be ascribed to its unreasonable treat-

ment. For every blow inflicted on the body rever-
berates a thousandfold in the spirit—and vice versa.
Before their death some of the most zealous of the
saints have confessed to pangs of conscience at their
tyrannical treatment of their "curse-laden" bodies.
"I was too hard on Brother Ass," St. Francis confessed when it was too late, and it was only then
that he invented the beautiful phrase "Brother
Body."

It follows that the dualism between spirit and body
must be replaced by a synthesis, if the ill-treated
body is not to avenge itself and make body and soul
alike diseased. "Today, more than ever," Francis
Thompson wrote, "we must love our bodies, instead
of hate them, and we must meet them with tender
patience. . . . As, in the Christian religion itself, love
is more and more taking the place of fear as the
driving force, might not the love of our bodies take
the place of hatred as the motive of our asceticism?
. . . Our task is not to suppress the energies of the
body but to cherish and tend them." If formerly man
was taught to mortify the instincts, in the new
"Christian Asceticism" of Hengstenberg we are
taught that "man is fundamentally right so long as
he takes up into his suffering his instincts along with
his bad inclinations. This suffering serves the preser-
vation of both spiritual and bodily health." In his
Mystique de la Terre the French Jesuit, Victor Pou-
cel, advises man to return to the good use of the
body: "Let us honor the body by allowing it to form
the first and firm foundation of our spiritual ascent."

The eye of the spirit has been dazzled by the sun
of God's holiness and made blind to the human
spheres that lie in darkness—which only wait for the

light of the spirit. The body as well as the spirit now yearns to tread the way of redemption that leads to Calvary. It too wants to expose itself to the scorching sun of God's holiness. Formerly spiritualization was the goal, now it is rather the molding of the whole of human life. The meaning of Christ's Incarnation for the Christian life on earth is being understood in a new light.

The Soul in the Striving for Holiness

The same process of change is repeated once again when the spiritual life emerges from the darkness and refuses any longer to be suppressed. Man's spiritual energies also groan under the tyranny of the intellect. They too want to be redeemed; otherwise they avenge themselves in the form of spiritual disease and stand in the way of spiritual aspiration. The soul is not something we can treat as we like. Eastern sages criticize the West for greatly neglecting the energies of the spirit. They accuse us of having developed the intellect at the expense of the soul. The result is the increase in the spiritual diseases known as neuroses. Neurosis is the typically modern disease; it has called forth an entirely new science, psychotherapy. Certain diseases can now be recognized for the first time as spiritual diseases and from their history we can derive laws for a hygiene and culture of the soul.

With the equipment of psychotherapy we can often discern, in the intercourse with our own souls, a dilettantism and a harmful experimentalism in a so-called striving for holiness. The result of these activities is "bad temper, the vice of the religious," insincerity, inhibitions, joylessness and the withering of the spiritual life; inner emptiness and sterility; self-disgust, restlessness, boredom, obsessions and scruples, leading sometimes to serious spiritual illness; depression, fear-neuroses, phobias, and so on. Those affected by these diseases of the spirit redouble their attempts to fight against the symptoms and to surmount the "temptations and hindrances" of the spiritual life by an intensified asceticism. But they merely fall deeper into the abyss of neurosis. The cause is purely natural, a spiritual indisposition which often expresses itself in physical symptoms. Primarily, however, the malady is due to a false attitude, the result of a false solution of an intellectual problem, and a wrong conception of holiness, not based on the natural view of man provided by anthropology. We propose, therefore, to investigate the connections between health and holiness by first deducing from the diseases of the spirit the laws for healthy spiritual striving. Then we shall show the health-bringing and health-preserving effects of the striving for holiness. For holiness is health.

St. Teresa of the Child Jesus had a compulsion-neurosis. She suffered from severe scruples for two years. How did that come about? In devout circles a definite conception of a saint was then current. He was considered the embodiment of all the virtues. The saint was devout, all his thoughts were devout, he saw his daily life and work from a devout point of view, all his intentions were devout. One outstanding characteristic was singled out from every type of saint, and all these individual characteristics fused into one ideal conception: the bravery of the martyr, the gentleness of the old, the chastity of the young, the modesty of the virgin, the solitude of the hermit, the innocence of the child. All these virtues and qualities were woven into a single garment and the soul in search of perfection was forced to wear it.

In her *History of a Soul* Teresa writes: "Whilst I was preparing for the solemn renewal of my first communion [exercises and spiritual renewal on the anniversary of the first communion] I was stricken by the terrible disease of scrupulousness. To understand it one must have been through this martyrdom oneself. It would be impossible for me to describe what I suffered for nearly two years. Every thought, every action became a source of fear and bewilderment. I only found peace after I had confided everything to Mary [her sister]. But that cost me a great deal, since I considered myself obliged to reveal every thought, however odd. Having got rid of my burden I enjoyed peace for a moment. But it vanished again like a flash and my martyrdom began anew." Her scruples made her so ill that she had to be taken away from boarding school when she was thirteen years old. At that time scruples were regarded as "vocational sufferings" for all seeking perfection. This disease was considered a regular and necessary evil, sent to test and tempt its victims, as if it were a genuine passport for the right way to perfection.

This suffering from obsessions is the vengeance the soul takes for its ill-treatment at the hands of the mind. Having been forced into a garment for which it was not suited, it now oppresses the mind with the obsession of guilt. Instead of stepping out briskly on the road to holiness, it is forced to mark time, constantly obsessed by the idea of sin. Redoubled eagerness in the striving for holiness merely aggravates the symptoms and leads in time to physical exhaustion. The morbid reaction of the soul against the urge to perfection indicates that it cannot live under such conditions, that the ideal of holiness pinches and impedes it, like a garment that is too skimpy and badly cut. Such a human being does not live his own life but another, one artificially forced upon him. He does not live his own truth but a lie. It is now possible to define spiritual disease: a man becomes spiritually ill when he lives against *his* truth. A man is spiritually healthy if he is living *his* truth. It follows that there is no universal way to perfection, but each must find his individual way. When the ideal of holiness represents the sum of all virtues, a lifeless plaster image is set up and the striving for holiness becomes mere imitation. But the real starting point should be the individual. Authentic sanctity is always bound up with an authentic human life, and hence with the uniqueness, with the limited talents and potentialities of the individual—which are *his* truth. It is wrong to say: "That is how I want to develop!" What one should say is: "What does God expect from me and my particular talents?"

Asceticism, then, must take the body into consideration because it follows laws of its own which cannot be infringed without prejudice to the unity of body and soul. But asceticism, we should remember, must also have regard for the laws of the soul, for the truth of the soul, which is an individual truth. A formation of life which, though it may be ideal, is foreign to the soul, impedes the formation of the individual personality, makes it a lie and leads to illness, to neurosis. Neurosis is, in fact, a cry for help from the suffering soul; it is a symptom of self-defense, like a physical inflammation, an impulse to health and therefore a signpost guiding a man to his own truth, helping him to meet himself.

Instead of fleeing from the illness the victim ought to plunge into himself, where the pressure of suffering is greatest, for there in his hidden depths he will find a treasure which is precisely that most needed for his recovery. A certain girl of twenty-six was living a blameless life. Always self-controlled and very devout, she followed in almost everything the precepts of her religion. But the following neurosis developed in her. She would wake up at night feeling she had fallen through ice and was in danger of drowning. In the great solitude into which she had sunk she experienced her own self as if separated from the surrounding world by a thick pane of glass. She continued to live among human beings, but it was as though she had no further contact, no further encounter with them. Instead, her solitude became peopled with gloomy ideas of guilt and depravity; she imagined that God had cast her out. When she slept, devilish dreams disturbed her; she was attacked by dreadful animals, against which she was powerless to make any defense. Terrified, she would awake and sit up for hours, fearing to dream again. The result was general exhaustion. She sought for help and comfort in religion, especially in the Bible, but this only made her condition worse. She had, as it were, really fallen through the ice, and the dark waters below had flooded her consciousness. Previously she had lived only consciously, rationalistically, making high intellectual demands on life. Always in control of herself, she had repressed all these dark, submerged, "unreasonable" things, and shut herself off from them. In the course of time an insulating layer had formed between the conscious and the unconscious. She had paid no heed to the unconscious and the instinctive. Instead of accepting them and wrestling with them, refining and cultivating them, she had left these layers of her soul to their own devices. But what is excluded from consciousness is not dead. It lives and carries on its mischief in the unconscious and pushes forward to the light of day until eventually the insulating layer is pierced. The conscious is flooded with dark, unspiritual things, and the terrified soul declares itself guilty and forsaken by God. And it is guilty—not before God, but before itself, because it has been living in opposition to the truth. It has tried to tread the path of holiness merely with the conscious mind and its powers; it has evaded the problems set by the unconscious. The soul includes both the conscious and the unconscious. Psychotherapy has altered the whole conception of the soul. The conscious, with the ego as its center, is only a part of the soul. The conscious superstructure is opposed by a substructure, by what Philipp Lersch has called the "endothymic basis." The truth of the soul is stretched out between the rational and the irrational, between Logos and Bios, between intellect and instinct. It follows that man discovers his truth and finds himself only when he has established the right balance between the conscious and the unconscious. It is untrue to say that it devolves solely on the conscious to take the lead in the solution of this problem. Often enough we are not aware of our own law of development. Does not intellect know what is growing up under its rule? Often the vital curve of the conscious life is in danger of departing from the natural life, from the "fertile soil of the soul" and hides its growth. A gulf arises between the conscious and the unconscious. The ego hangs in the air, paralyzed with fear. It has been going its own ways—reasonable ways, it may be, and devout—but it has thereby come into conflict with the truths of the blood which are written into the unconscious. The natural laws of the psyche are infringed. The basic facts of life and the soul are disregarded and our lives become unnatural. The lower strata of the soul are comparable to a natural organism, growing like a plant in accordance with its own laws. The spirit, striving for perfection, all too easily and swiftly cramps this growth instead of respecting the wonderful nature of the soul. The mind needs to be humble, to admit that it must lay down the scepter of government from time to time; it cannot and must not determine itself, but hearken to the secret growth in the depths of the soul.

In most neuroses the "natural soul" is buried. Our Christian education, our asceticism and striving for perfection tend all too much to repress and eliminate the natural soul. There is still no affirmation of our total human nature; the deeper levels of the soul are still excluded from Christian penetration. The defection from the Church in the West is not merely a rejection of Christian faith; it is partly due to a feeling that the Church does not accept the whole of human nature, that inside the Church the deeper levels of the personality cannot breathe and live. The psychotherapist works where spiritual suffering is greatest in the modern world; he comes to see all too plainly that ministers of religion often do not understand the souls committed to their care and that the "natural kingdom of the soul" has not yet found a home in the life of the Church. But the hopeful fact is nevertheless impressed on him that although the liberation of the natural soul binds man nearer to the world and the earth, the new outlook which this inspires is followed by a fuller and loftier, a deeper and more vital religious life. One often hears it said that it is only after this change has taken place that a feeling arises for the preciousness of the God-man; that the symbolism of the liturgy acquires a more vivid significance; that the life of prayer becomes vital, an authentic dialogue with the Divine Thou.

To live a spiritually healthy life one must find one's own truth, and to find one's own truth the natural soul must be laid bare; one must consciously come to terms with the irrational forces within oneself, incorporating them into the total life of the soul but never allowing them a perfectly free rein. The problem is to build the natural sphere harmoniously into the total human personality. The doctor concerned with the wholeness of the soul knows that a man finds himself, comes to himself only when he lays his soul bare. Stripping the soul is an essential part of the hygiene and culture of the soul. It makes the personality deeper, clearer and more embracing. Laying the soul bare is a form of loyalty to one's own ground plan. If the striving for perfection is to keep man's soul in wholeness and health, he will have to be led along the path of self-unfolding. A Christian formation that slows up, or even prevents this total uncovering of the lower strata of the spirit, leads to spiritual impoverishment and paralysis, since all spiritual vitality flows from the depths, out of which the conscious mind rises up like an island. Spiritual atrophy leads to disease, especially in the case of rich and valuable natures. When the soul does not live its own truth, the vision of God's truth also becomes clouded, for spiritual disease involves our whole thinking, our feeling and willing, and even what our senses perceive.

How serious and urgent is the problem of a change in our whole attitude to the spiritual life is clear when a Catholic psychotherapist writes as a responsible Christian: "It seems to be extremely desirable that the minister of religion should make himself familiar with the outlook of psychotherapy throughout his work. This would make possible a complete rebirth of the cure of souls and prevent incalculable harm." It is the task of a Christian philosophy of life to rethink man's wholeness, naturally and supernaturally. One chapter in this philosophy is man's relationship to himself. Our souls have at their disposal a certain measure of energy, but it varies greatly from one individual to another. The soul is charged with this energy like an accumulator; part of it is at the disposal of the conscious mind; the rest operates in the unconscious. There is a constant to-and-fro in the soul which can be compared to an energic system relatively closed. ("Relatively closed" since we do not know if an influx of energy is possible from the biological sphere.) The to-and-fro of tension is, therefore, an energic process and satisfies the natural laws of energy. When in nature an amount of energy disappears—in coal, for example—the same quantum appears in another form of energy—for example, as heat. Moreover, the transformation of one form of energy into another is possible only when there is a tension, such as that produced by differences of height, as when water power is converted into electricity. These two laws, the conservation of energy and the law of entropy, also apply to the dynamics of the spiritual economy. When we attend to a problem with the conscious mind, we withdraw the spiritual energy we need for this purpose from another sphere of interest. To do one thing thoroughly, every other task must be laid on one side. If the religious life claims a great deal of energy, it must be withdrawn from other spheres of the spirit. Up to a certain point we can even drain off energy from the unconscious and feed it to the conscious. It is clear that there are limits to this conscious striving. In a healthy spiritual household the balance is restored automatically after a time by the unconscious reabsorbing the energy lost to the conscious.

If those who strive for spiritual perfection sometimes complain about a spiritual emptiness and dryness (which is not identical with the mystical "Dark Night" of the soul) this may become outwardly apparent as an incapacity for any devout feelings. But they are in reality passing through a necessary and health-preserving reaction to the spirit. The conscious part of the spirit is being emptied of vital energy; it is tired, sluggish and desolate. There must be a pause in the activity of the consciousness. During this pause the vital energy that has disappeared from the conscious is active in the unconscious. We imagine that there is a deadly emptiness within us, yet all the time the soul is working hard in the unconscious. After a time the results of this spiritual effort in the depths of the soul are seen in a new access of energy to the conscious spirit. This vital energy is gradually released again by the unconscious and provides the conscious with a new stimulus. It has renewed and replenished itself with images in "God's cellar"; it has been born again in the womb of the deep places of the spirit. The intervening time has not been lost; it has been a creative interval. If anyone fights against the process and persists in maintaining a purely conscious approach to it, he falls victim to neurosis. In such a neurosis the force of the laws of energy can be observed as under a magnifying glass. A natural balance is impossible, because the conscious resists; therefore the energy-complexes make themselves independent, as it were, in the unconscious; they attack the conscious in the rear and produce the most peculiar symptoms.

We repeat that the conscious is only part of a comprehensive energic system. The will cannot rule arbitrarily and depart from the laws governing this system; otherwise, it will be hollowed out. Energy will be drawn away from it by the unconscious. The soul is a natural organism with self-driving powers in a hidden entelechy.

But here we must pause. If this were true, man's self-determination would seem to be undermined, all intellectual and spiritual endeavor would cease, asceticism would be an unnatural martyrdom and the dignity of the person lost! But it is only in spiritual illness that man becomes a victim to the laws of energy. Normally the conscious has its place within the process of natural growth, but it occupies a special position in the total economy of the spirit. On the one hand, it must entrust itself to the inner workings of the unconscious, but it is also able to rise superior to them and even exercise a decisive influence on the direction of the whole personality. Ethical aspiration, decision, sacrifice and self-control are still possible. We are simply trying to point to a new way of spiritual authenticity. What we have to avoid is the error of imagining that we can do whatever we like with ourselves; for then the living will becomes sheer anarchic willfulness, even in the religious sphere, and fruitful activity become empty bustle. The true art of life is to find the middle course between indulgence and austerity. The conscious must learn to come to terms with the unconscious. Then there will be room for spiritual discipline and freedom for the creative development of one's own personal nature. In the interplay of spiritual forces the conscious is not cast for the role of tyrant. It can best enforce its will when it works like the index of a balance. Then it has power to act decisively. It needs real practice and ascetic discipline before the conscious can find its true center. Like all life, spiritual life develops in wavy lines. It has its ups and downs. When we find ourselves in a valley, and the conscious feels empty and hollow, we should not tire ourselves out with prayer and meditation and spiritual exercises. We must rather observe the times of spiritual pregnancy and delivery. This entering into one's own rhythm means a co-operating with nature so as to gain the strength and impetus required for going beyond it. It means cultivating nature in order to surpass it. The ego is, as it were, in a boat on the river of the unconscious. It is impossible to row against the stream —that leads to exhaustion and spiritual disease—but both banks can be reached *with* the stream, which means encountering one's real self. That is the central position between frivolous experimentation with the self and the weakling's dread of life.

If anyone has already yielded to the suspicion that we have been speaking against asceticism, against the laws of morality, it should now have become clear that we are not concerned with setting up a moral code that decrees what we should be, but rather with delineating a moral psychology. We want to show how the Christian can become what he is intended to be: a saint. Asceticism will always remain, because it is necessary; its nature remains constant, but its outward form changes; it must serve modern men seeking for a way to live a saintly Christian life without becoming spiritually ill. It is possible to strive for holiness without becoming spiritually ill; or, to put it less pretentiously, Christianity and health are not mutually exclusive. Truth is the measure and power of both. Admittedly, to assert this implies that all teachers of the spiritual life are called upon to find ways of guiding the irrational in a Christian direction and to point to ways in which the energies of the vital sphere can be conveyed to the sphere of conscious faith.

II
THE THREE DIVINE VIRTUES AND THEIR INFLUENCE ON HEALTH

Truth is the sun in the life of the soul. Truth determines its health, which is why we were able to say that to be spiritually healthy is to live one's own truth. Simple as this statement sounds, it nevertheless appears to be dangerous. Does not "our truth" also contain elements of evil? Are these to be "lived" as well? Is man to be allowed to expose his whole nature? Will not this bring him into conflict with the moral law of Christianity? Or, to put it another way: What happens when the *veritas naturalis*—the natural truth of a man, his personal qualities—strives upwards and meets the *Veritas supranaturalis* which shines forth from Christ, the Image of God, the Truth that comes down from above? What happens when they meet? The law of original sin and the mystery of redemption and the cross stand revealed. These truths of revelation are part of man's truth and necessary to complete it.

We propose to investigate these problems practically rather than theoretically by studying three phenomena in which human nature is exposed to the influence of Revelation. The three phenomena are related to the divine virtues of faith, hope and love, which exercise a healing and sanctifying influence on the spiritual life. We here come to the meeting-place of virtue and natural spiritual power, the point where nature and supernature interact and the healing power of Grace *(gratia sanans)* is proven.

The three divine virtues are divine energies. At baptism they are implanted in the ground of the soul. They are at the same time the comprehensive expression of man's striving for the Godlike life, for holiness. They bind man to the goal of his spiritual striving, to God, to Truth and Life. They are our answer to God, but at the same time they are the power and source from which we are able to give this answer. Faith is the ability to think with Christ. It is an entering into mental communion with Him; it is a participation in the truth of God. In hope the Christian enters into the unfolding purpose of Christ's life; it is a participation in the divine will, a self-adjustment to the divine plan. Love is a flowing into the rhythm of God's love, a participation in the Agape in which human love can alone find redemption and healing. It is, in fact, our task to bring our natural abilities within the range of these divine gifts in order that they may all be slowly recast. This is the slow process of Christian metamorphosis—the way of sanctification. Our thinking must undergo a slow change, our intentions adapt themselves to the promised hope, our love allow itself to be redeemed by the fire of God's love on the cross. This lifelong process of conversion acts like the constantly repeated passing of a magnet over iron, so that in time all the molecules group themselves in one direction. We now propose briefly to sketch the effects of the process on fear, on the growth to maturity in man and on his sexual life.

Fear and the Virtue of Faith

Fear plays a tremendous part in man's spiritual life. Like the climate, it can influence the smallest detail. For the psychotherapist it is the mysteriously and secretly active nucleus of almost every neurosis. The fear motive is concealed behind the most contrary phenomena, such as a mania for work or virtue, for piety or pedantry. Jaspers writes of a possibly unprecedented fear of life as the secret attendant of modern man. It was thought at first that this was merely a sign of degeneration, a defect of modern civilization. But existential philosophy has mercilessly exposed the fact that fear is part of the truth in human existence. For the theology of Scholasticism the fearful was always a reality of human existence. The more grown-up Western man becomes, the more conscious and better able to see through illusions, the more he comes to the limits of his own potentialities, the more plain the naked truth appears—and of that he is justifiably afraid. Now that Western man is at the end of his intellectual tether and the polyphony of philosophy is silent, he is becoming aware of the monotonously regular and uncontrollable murmuring that whispers through his soul— the murmuring of fear. Often he does not realize as yet that this noise is actually fear; he tries to escape from it. But it is not man that holds fear, fear holds man. Fear is the encounter with the nothingness from which we have arisen and near to which we remain. How does modern man solve the problems which fear sets him? He tries to become evil; he does evil in order to create a cause for his fear and to be able to see through it. Yet, even when he makes up his mind to do the most evil things and tries to make them stick in the neck of fear and kill it, fear still swallows the worst he can do and its murmurings continue to echo in his heart. "The dangerous thing about this world," Max Picard writes, "is that the greatest evil seems small compared with fear." Man tries to escape from fear—but fear overtakes him always. He flees from himself; he is no more at home but a mere lodger within himself. The eyes that ought to shine with a radiant light and say: "Here is man, here am I!" are only will-o'-the-wisps in the face of man on the run. Man is split in two by fear: he is, physically, and yet he is no longer; inwardly he has fled from himself and he flees till he gives himself up. The further he flees, the louder becomes the sound of fear.

Other ways of consciously meeting fear have been described. Fritz Klatt has introduced us to Goethe and Rilke as teachers in this difficult problem. Goethe, though adhering to no religious faith, died in the pious consciousness that everything must be as it is. Of all men who have ever lived, Rilke (according to Klatt) made the greatest advance towards a solution of the problem. He held out in darkness and uncertainty to the end; in his poems all things flourish, in the neighborhood of nothingness and fear, as in a rich autumnal beauty; the preciousness of Being is felt above the abyss of nothingness. Klatt goes on to say that there is a hidden strength in fear and terror. In the moment of imminent death, in war for instance, a power suddenly comes over a man which causes him to love the inevitable and even the cessation of his own life. This fervor of self-surrender to an unavoidable darkness, albeit an impersonal darkness, is creative. Fear seems to have been vanquished in this heroic and stoical attitude to life. But in fact it has merely withdrawn to the innermost chamber of the heart. In sleep the door of the chamber is opened and fear invades the sleeper's dreams. "Almost all the dreams of these adventurous hearts are dreams of fear." So Josef Pieper writes with reference to Ernst Jünger. How little all the efforts to endure fear avail is clearly realized by the psychotherapist as he observes the increase in spiritual sickness of which fear is almost always the root cause.

Such is the situation which Christ meets when He says:

> . . . do not be anxious for your life, what you shall eat; nor yet for your body, what you shall put on. . . . Look at the birds of the air: they do not sow, or reap, or gather into barns . . . yet your heavenly Father feeds them (Matt. 6:25-26).

This is no rash consolation, implying that Providence will care for the children of God. To interpret it thus means that one has failed to penetrate to its deeper meaning. It is not a word of consolation at all, but a crucial prohibition. The sentence "I forbid you to fret" does not mean "I will take your worries upon myself and then all will be well with you." On the contrary, it removes the ultimate safeguards from man, it exposes him to total fear. We are to live as carefree as the birds. "See how the birds of the air never sow or reap or gather grain into barns"—but we know that not all birds find their grain, that some freeze and die of hunger in the snow. That is the **decisive** point. Ultimately it is quite unimportant whether a man dies of hunger, whether he is well or ill. God has not undertaken to see that His disciples fare well in this life. The human situation could not, in fact, be demonstrated more clearly than in this injunction of Christ. It almost makes one dizzy to be forced to look into this fearful abyss. But we are not impelled into this stupefying insecurity simply to sink resignedly into the inevitable darkness. That is falsehood; it is against the intentions of life itself. In the midst of this fear we are to have the courage to let ourselves go and put our trust in another whom we have never seen, to seek an invisible hand, to believe in a heart that has passed through every one of our fears and now reigns above as Christ the Lord. God has promised that whoever serves Him will not be lost. To let oneself go and in the very midst of fear to trust another, of whom one knows only by faith, is to be redeemed from fear. Fear calls forth the desire for security, but faith demands that the heart should abandon itself to the unknown God, to a Person. Insofar as he refuses this surrender and sinfully rejects the faith, unredeemed man exposes himself to fear with all its imperilings of health. Here lies the slender channel where sin leads to disease. It is impossible to investigate the connection between sin and disease in detail. But that there is a connection is just as much a fact as that faith liberates from fear, with its disease-bearing effects, and itself bestows health. The paralysis of fear is changed into the thrill of expectation at the coming of the Lord. For His appearance will be sudden and unexpected.

Spiritual Maturation and the Virtue of Hope

Our bodies are subject to a development that allows us no rest. They drive us irresistibly forward from birth to death. Through our bodies we are the slaves of a current that bears us past many shores. After a short stay we have to leave each of them. We are driven forwards, as Jaspers says, by "biological factors independent of the individual person." The child becomes a girl, a mother, an old woman. We grow up, flourish, reach a climax and then decline towards old age and death. This life-process confronts our souls with a great problem, the problem of maturing. Each new stage in life demands a parting from the previous one. The realm of childhood has to be left behind if youth is to develop, and youth disappears as life claims the adult. The aging must put up with being pensioned off; they must let youth carry on the work of the world. The biological process forces us on from stage to stage. But the tendency of the spirit is against leaving the old in order to receive the new. Spiritual development does not always keep pace with the biological course of life. What an effort of readjustment is required of the small child, for example, when a brother or sister is born and pushes itself between that child and the mother! There is a conflict in the child's soul. The joy over the arrival of the new baby is at odds with grief at incipient detachment from the mother! The discord is repeated in the conflict between the desire to remain a child and the desire to grow up, and— from the parents' point of view, this time—between parental love and the necessity to release the children as they grow up; between wanting to remain young and accepting the responsibilities of motherhood. To bestow life on a child is, in the depths of the soul, a renunciation in favor of the new generation and requires a surrender of the ego, a spiritual maturing. The numerous spiritual disturbances connected with pregnancy and motherhood have their root in a failure to surrender the ego. With men this task of spiritual maturing is bound up with their professional life. The crisis often comes about the age of 42, when a man's career has reached its zenith and is destined henceforward to proceed in a straight line.

In its analysis of dreams, psychotherapy has taken a look at what goes on in the depths of the spirit when we are forced to proceed from one inward stage to another. An eight-year-old girl dreams that her mother is taking her into a wood. She leaves the child in the middle of the wood and the child suffers great anxiety for its mother, since it knows that its mother must die. But it is, of course, not the mother that must die, but the child's dependence on its mother. In the depths of its soul the necessary loosening of the ties binding the child to its mother is felt as a death and finds corresponding expression in the dream. The old must die if the new is to be born. This law of "Die and become" is fulfilled in every process of spiritual maturing. In the unconscious every departure from one stage in life is a death.

During a spiritual change, a mortal fear is experienced in the unconscious—and if man resists it tenaciously his spiritual life stands still, grows paralyzed and diseased.

In the midst of this discord and conflict between the physical urge to go forward and the shrinking fear of the spirit, man encounters tidings of a future world-event. The message proclaims that the day will come when God will emerge upon the scene of creation from His mysteriously hidden life. That will be a day of shocks and crisis, but at the same time a day of bliss. Then the promise will be fulfilled that God will reign among the children of men, that He will do all things well and devote all His powers of kingship to their good. An age of world-renewal will dawn; there will be a new heaven and a new earth. A superficial conception of this hope can all too easily mislead the Christian into living merely with his mind on the future and not taking the present seriously. This typically Christian danger of disregarding whole stages of life is a religious short cut. The people who indulge in it are hollow. Their precocity produces only phantom fruit; it is barren and vain.

The genuine Christian virtue of hope is no mere knowledge but a gift from God, an event in the soul. A change in life of the spirit is awakened by the proclamation of a future event. In Bergengruen's novel *In Heaven as on Earth,* he shows how the proclamation of an impending event can permeate all a person's thinking, all his feeling and willing. A message is a reality, an active influence. A girl receives a message telling her that her betrothed is coming home. The whole aspect of her surroundings will be changed for her; she will see her environment differently because she herself has become different. Every object will seem to tell her that he is coming soon. Rejuvenated, possessed of new strength, she will overcome difficulties more easily, for nothing can assail her now. Everything is focused on the coming day of his arrival. Yet in spite of thinking of the future she lives in the present: all her work is done carefully, for everything must pass the test of his scrutiny. She has become one who waits. Her sense of time has changed: she lives for the future, but in the present. The future has been absorbed into the present. Her whole life is a "waiting." The Christian must also be one who waits. The exciting message, with which Christ begins and completes His activity, declares that God—the Awful, the Holy One, the Father—is about to enter the world. The constant menace, urgency and joyful expectation of this "early coming" influence those who believe in it. It changes the character of their time on earth and gives it a new quality. For the believer, his life in time will be influenced by the coming of Christ. Waiting for the coming of God is not merely a filling in of time but a being filled with God, with the divine gift of hope. One must submit to the transforming power of the "last things" and see oneself as one who waits for the Lord. Then the soul will open its eyes and look into the face of this world's truth. For all creatures are waiting with man. As we Christians are already being fed with the energies of the coming age, and live thereon, so the tidings of the consummation of time must also transform our thinking and go on to permeate our feelings, until all the depths of mind and spirit are slowly reorientated toward the coming of the Lord. In this long process nature surrenders itself to the divine gift of hope in order to be filled with the whole spirit of Christ.

Thus our souls are drawn by the future as are our bodies. The physical and the spiritual processes have this in common that they are both *in via*. To avoid stoppages, the spiritual life must flow into the future undisturbed. Provided it does not skip over any intermediate stage—that would be against the purposes of God—the maturing spirit will pass the dangerous reefs of spiritual disease and preserve an easy and steady flow which alone can bestow health on the soul. The virtue of hope makes man free for the process of maturing, for a growing into the full stature of Christ. In addition, it gives the spirit the elasticity which is expressed in the charming youthfulness of the great saints. Nothing guarantees and establishes "eternal youth" so much as the theological virtue of hope.

Man's Love Life and the Virtue of Love

The energy of love, called Eros, presents man with what is probably his most difficult problem in his intercourse with himself and with God. Its importance becomes plain when we remember that in order to become fully conscious the personality needs to look with love on another person, on a Thou. In love, the personality comes to life. It is here that man learns who he is in his innermost heart. Human personality includes sexual love—not the erotic, but the Eros. It is here that man is most sensitive and most vulnerable. The deepest and most secretive suffering is based all too often on love and its problems. The many sexual neuroses show how few signposts there are to help man build into the personality the energy of sexual love. The experience of the psychotherapists has often led them to criticize Christianity for making a false assessment of sexual love, for trying to repress it. And it is a fact that so-called religious people often do display great uncertainty in this sphere and an excessive apprehension about everything connected with sex. Many sexual neuroses can be traced back to education in a religious house. Jung reproaches the Church for not distinguishing between Eros (love between the sexes) and Sexus (the sexual instinct), and for an attitude to sexual matters comparable only to the wholesale condemnation, in the Middle Ages, of all financial transactions. Eros has been dragged into the mud along with Sexus and been loaded with a centuries-old guilt. It has acquired a bad conscience. Nietzsche says that Christianity gave Eros poison to drink. One often has the impression that chastity is the central concern of Christian morals; Christianity seems to have changed from a religion of love into a religion of chastity. It would be very easy to quote examples, right up to the present day. But in this sphere, too, it is still true that "Holiness is health." The Christian way of life is able to guide the sexual life along healthy lines. In other words, the divine virtue of love, the Agape, can redeem the Eros. To be sure, Eros must tread the way of the cross, and modern man is the incarnation of loneliness because he refuses to find and take this way. Eros and religion are dependent on one another. Whoever separates them and sows enmity between them creates a schism between human and divine love. Where Eros and religion are mutually exclusive, Eros becomes vulgar and religion cold. Eros sinks to the level of animal lust and religion becomes numbed. For it is Eros that loosens the ground of the soul, makes the spirit soft and malleable. It cultivates the energies of enthusiasm in the soul without which the religious life grows languid. But where Eros and religion combine, Eros is ennobled, spiritualized, transfigured and, in return, gives vitality to religion. They have much in common and might well reach out a hand of welcome to each other. They have the same mortal enemy: egotism. Love will never flourish unless everything is seen from the point of view of the loved one; hence love is a preparation for what religion demands: self-surrender to God. Eros and religion both live on devotion to another. Both are intent on the same goal, redemption from the ego. In love for man and love for God the yearning heart watches out for the other who can liberate it from the confinement of the single person, break through the wall of isolation, and fill it with the gift of communion.

But religion and Eros are also distinct. Not in the sense that they are enemies or rivals, but in that Eros is able to lead the spirit towards religion. Every love —according to Max Scheler—is love for God taking a rest by the wayside. But whereas the love of God promises redemption, Eros has no fulfillment to give. Behind its motive-power there is only a saddening premonition of unity. Eros is a being of death, *Eros thanatos;* it does not die, but it is always dying. Divine love, on the other hand, leads through death to redemption. We do not mean that Eros should be killed, shunned or repressed. That is not the way to shape the sexual life in a religious sense; it is the way to spiritual disease and neurosis. Charles Péguy has indicated what a blind alley this is bound to be:

"Because they love no one, they imagine they love God." A serious self-deception! No evasion of suffering is possible in the "adventure of love." But God helps the Christian in this his greatest suffering with a gift of His love which contains redemption within itself: the Eucharist. The life of Christ Himself is contained in the Eucharist. The power of love of the God-man on the cross absorbed death unto itself. But God roused the dead body to new life and filled it with divine love. Thus both His dying and His resurrection are contained in the body of the Lord. In the Eucharist, Eros and Agape meet. The energy of divine love penetrates our exhausted, yielding capacity for love. The divine virtue of love is a flowing into the love-rhythm of God. This rhythm fills us with new life and brings us once more into communion with others. The suffering of love, in and outside marriage, becomes a fountain of active love in the service of others. The relationship to the other sex is now borne by an unembarrassed confronting and genuine communion even without any sexual association. Graciously the Lord turns our passion on to Himself when we bring our love to the cross. On the cross Agape takes Eros into her arms.

Let us sum up by recounting a vivid dream. The subject was a woman of thirty-eight who was startled out of the quietness of her monotonous and already rather meaningless existence by a human encounter which awakened her to the fullness of love. In accordance with the law of the Church she had to renounce this love. There was shown her, in her trouble, the way to the loving, sacrificial mind of Christ, and the meaning of the Eucharist. Then, after a long period of suspense, she had the following dream:

I was standing with my sister in the North room of our one-time home in M. and looking through the door into the South room, in which mother was distributing something holy. I noticed how some of it was falling on the floor. It looked like a fragment of the host. But she did not notice it. So I went to the spot where I thought the holy fragment must be lying, sought for it on my knees and found a piece of reddish egg-shell and beside it the tiny particle of an egg. I recognized this as the holy thing and at first did not dare to take it in my hand. But it had to be picked up and I did so with reverent care. Then I noticed that a faint streak of light was flashing across the palm of my hand. Then a little ball of light moved inside it like a tiny sun. Suddenly the light grew into yellowish golden flames, which leapt up out of my hands, and, overcome with awe, I raised my hands to heaven like a sacrificial bowl of fire. The room became bright and suddenly I saw a crucifix on the wall above me, the head of which, like the golden fire in my hands, shone ever more brightly until it attained the inconceivable radiance of the face of Christ. Enraptured, and at the same time deeply affected by this sight, I surrendered myself entirely. It was an experience beyond words. But the bowl of my hands with the sacrificial fire was the symbol of my glowing prayer. Gradually the transfigured head of Christ faded and the flame in my hands died out. I rose and went into the North room, back to my sister, and awoke.

Dreams like that occur perhaps once or twice in a lifetime, and even then only if there is a strong power of imagery in the soul. This dream therefore serves merely as an illustration and a summary. Dreams rise from the depths of our being and show in images what we are really like. The transformation which took place in the woman who had this dream was genuine, not merely deliberately willed but a happening in the depths of her soul. The unconscious finds wonderful images. The mother and the egg point to her sexuality, to her natural destiny as a wife and mother. She had not evaded the inner urge, but had accepted it as a gift. She picked up the egg. Flames leapt up out of it—painful and destructive flames, purifying and transforming. The image of fire denotes transformation. In the dream she was wholly surrendered, nothing in her tried to ward off the burning and transforming power of her suffering love and dying. Then the mystery was revealed to her in the face of Christ on the cross, in the same fiery glow. God works in the fire, in suffering. She went back to her sister; she took the transformation for granted; she was now openly free to devote herself to her sister—and her sisters.

Admittedly, this struggle was also bound up with a physical crisis. But after the physical crisis had been overcome the spiritual change led to a fresh, healthy life, filled with new meaning. She now lived her truth. Love had brought her to the unfolding of her own being. Her religion had become fluid and alive again; she radiated new life in the community. Holiness is health. Her problem is a universal one: how to unite the whole of human nature with Christianity, how to attempt to form a holy and Christlike life whilst affirming all the energies of the personality. The problem and the task is how to be wholly worldly and wholly devoted to God. This is the tension that was endured on the cross alone. The paradox of the two statements: "Holiness is health" and "Holiness leads to disease" is resolved only on the cross. Through the cross of Christ, holiness and health become one.

2:　PSYCHOTHERAPY AND PASTORAL CARE

The change in the structure of man is with ever-increasing urgency forcing exponents of pastoral care to face the problem of *humanitas christiana*. Whenever modern man's religious feelings are appealed to, his nature revolts unless allowances are made for *humanitas christiana*. He is unable to comprehend religion solely on the basis of some pious feeling. There is no assurance that a religious disposition brings with it all the concomitant aspects of a man already subdued by the authority of educator and pastor. Rather, human nature is so secularized, so independently-oriented, that it can find its way into the religious sphere only when it is itself taken seriously and directly appealed to: then, indeed, it reacts with that decisiveness and strength that can only be found in a genuinely religious life. Pastoral care, therefore, requires an intimate knowledge of human nature, because the pastor must demonstrate how this nature—*humanitas*—can obtain the grace which alone can penetrate and transform it into *humanitas christiana*.

There are parallels between these two problems: pastoral care, on the one hand, and that intellectual development of our times which is characterized by the search for the essence of man. Depth psychology has opened up new dimensions of human life. Increased knowledge of the depth of the soul has colored research in anthropology because depth psychology, building on the body-soul unity, has reached beyond the life of the soul and thus views the whole man. It is depth psychology and, at the moment, psychotherapy—its most usable branch— which are to be investigated regarding their significance for pastoral care.

Such an enterprise is, of course, faced with difficulties which are partly inherent by nature. Depth psychology stems from psychotherapy which originates in sickness: it views the neurotic person and leads him back to wholeness which is equivalent to humaneness, since neurosis, a discord within oneself, must be regarded as a falsification of life. Viewed in this way, psychotherapy, for the pastor, is a science serving a special task, the treatment of the psychically sick. Thus, it is necessary to separate the theoretical knowledge gained by depth psychology, and the practical achieved through psychotherapy, from the stigma of "sickness" so that pastoral care can attain its rightful place in matters of the Church. Pastoral care rightly protests against seeing man only from the angle of sickness and demands advice applicable to the life of the healthy, normal man.

A desirable consequence of the necessity for rethinking the newly acquired knowledge of interior life is the fact that psychotherapy is no longer dictating the rules of thinking. This opens the way for a truly Christian inquiry. If we were to succeed in ordering the new sciences into Christian anthropology, we would find a new and broader foundation for *humanitas christiana,* and pastoral care would become more of an objective help. Outside the Church, depth psychology is leading to an everincreasing "psychologication" of all spheres of life, including the religious one. Only a true order in the structure of the Christian idea of man (which means inserting depth psychology into the thinking of the Church) can counteract this slow poisoning. The following paragraphs will point up the direction which needs to be taken in this regard.

II

The essence of Christianity is the personal relationship between God and man. Expressed in the manner of Revelation: God calls man—and man must reply.[1] Thus, everything human, according to its being, is subordinated and directed toward a Thou. In sum, every human endeavor should follow a dynamic motion of answering and giving, and nothing human should be excluded from this primitive happening. We must, therefore, search for a place in the nature of man which contains all the facets of his being, representing his whole existence and expressing the core of his persona. By its responsible "Yes" this core of the persona answers God's call in the form of the whole man. This basic happening would elevate *humanitas* into *humanitas christiana*.

The concept of the Self in depth psychology presents a complex of meanings and relations which can satisfy all the demands of a core of the person capable of religious feeling. The Self is a synthesis of the conscious and unconscious, the rational and irrational, of Logos and Bios: it takes hold of a man as a body-soul unity. The Self is the expression of man unified in every stratum, the "word" of all humanity. In it man is existent, and unified existence is contained in it.

---

[1] Cf. Karl Rahner, *Hörer des Wortes* (Munich, 1963).

The use of the concept of Self, however, in the Christian idea of man, must be differentiated from its use in depth psychology. C. G. Jung,[2] father of the concept of Self, considers the Self as sufficient unto itself and even burdens it with the attribute of the divine. For Christian pastoral care, the Self is a purely psychic element which has to provide the creature's answer to God the Creator. Depth psychology can thus furnish only the "raw material" of the Self which has to be refined in the Christian form of living.[3]

Through his theoretical agnosticism, Jung puts a ceiling, as it were, on the concept of the Self, sealing it hermetically against an upper world of metaphysics, enclosing it like a flower in a hothouse. He considers expressions of the divine the hothouse fantasies and dreams of his patients' "self-realizations." In these self-realizations apologetics may find a key to the various mystical experiences of all non-Christian religions and may be able to explain the outward parallel with the Christian mystical experience. The basic human material remains the same for both. In the Christian affirmation of faith the Self is opened up, above itself, and thus directed to its aim, the union with God. Self and affirmation of faith belong to each other like instrument and tone.

Consequently, it is the task of pastoral care to help the individual to "Self realization," and to see to it that the Self can give the affirmation of faith in full

---

[2] See C. G. Jung, *Collected Works,* VII, Bollingen Series (New York, Pantheon).

[3] Cf. Goldbrunner, *Individuation* (Notre Dame: University of Notre Dame Press, 1964).

freedom. Both tasks are interdependent and are brack-
eted together in the concept of *spiritual guidance*
which turns to everything human to make it sub-
servient to the divine. Thus the sluggish blood cir-
culation of religious life is speeded up from a languid
"holding on to truths" to a significant spirituality.
Spiritual guidance eases the tension between man and
God and shows the way for the Christian to live in
the world and yet belong to God. The shopworn concept of spiritual guidance takes on new content,
meaning and human dignity. Through this situation
pastoral care and pastoral psychology are confronted
with new tasks.

III

(1) The most important task is a presentation of
the new concept of the psyche which shows a synthesis
of all strata of the soul in the Self. Its main intention
is educational. The reader should be able to immerse
himself in depth psychology, an existential science.
It cannot be studied or grasped only from theory—
its recognition depends on a "becoming man." The
misinterpretations, refusals of recognition, and attacks against the new psychology are mostly due to
its being approached with the tools of rationalistic
thinking, which causes misunderstanding. If the
psyche is more than consciousness and rationality,
if rationality and irrationality are united in the Self
as in a superimposed third element, it is necessary
to assign to that Self a special category of psychic
being—the personal. He who studies depth psychology
cannot help but submit himself to the process of self-
realization.

(2) If depth psychology is to be accepted within
the theological thinking of the Church, the new

science must be explored philosophically and theologically. It consists to a great extent in searching out the connections with tradition and the teaching of the Church Fathers on spiritual life. Furthermore, one must see how far the scholastic concepts apply to the newly perceived realms of the life of the soul. We will find astonishingly close parallels to the new ways of self-realization by referring to the teaching of the Church Fathers, to the teachings of spiritual writers of all times, and especially to those of the French Oratorians. Sometimes it seems as if the sporadic and unsystematic knowledge of the soul's life, stored away in the palaces of Church tradition, could be collected and organized through the instrument of depth psychology, because the one has such close bearing on the other.

(3) The presentation of a new psychology culminates in pointing out a way of self-realization. The markers on this way are:

> The Ego
> Sex
> Community
> Religion

A doctrine of the Christian way of life will show the Christian reorientation of these markers, or layers of being, in the spiritual life.

The Ego which has shed the wrappings of untruth is the basic premise for a religious life which cannot flourish except in authenticity. The education of love life lends vitality to the I-Thou relationship with God and prevents unreal projection into religious feelings. Proving oneself in community life opens a way to fulfillment as life's requirements increase. For God's riches are mirrored in the fullness of reality.

Religious disposition, the organs for feeling the tremendous and the fascinating, the Dionysian powers, claim fulfillment but also demand their own taming. Confrontation with the gospel will delineate Christianity sharply from all other religions, an indication of which may be seen in the confrontation of "Dance" and "Word." The religious expression of man as a natural being is a Dionysian dance and intoxication in various degrees, from the orgy to mere esthetic hovering in "pious" or awestruck reticence for the inscrutable mystery. How often are these things mistaken for Christianity! In contrast, revealed religion speaks in the sacred sobriety of the "word" and forms molds into which the Dionysian forces of man can pass as through a crucible and find redemption. The Catholic liturgy is a classic example for the Christianization of religious disposition.

For the attainment of the four stages to self-realization to serve as a practical guide, two demands must be fulfilled:

First, a theory of self-education has to be worked out, the aim of which is not the promise of self-control —as usual— but the Christian life of the fully realized nature. Self-education means a Christian penetration of all layers of being.

Second, this is the foundation for a theory of spiritual life. It starts with the first steps, such as recollection and reading of the scriptures, and ascends to the forecourts of mysticism, where, for instance, the spiritual senses are located. The experiences of depth psychology, strange as it seems, incite them, encourage them to drink deep, not only from the wellsprings of the soul but also from the sources of mysticism. The modern Christian desires not only to be "pious" but to live as a Christian, that is, to live a spiritual life. How many priests are actually able to lead the way, or at least advise and interpret in those cases—and they are not rare—where a Christian has already unknowingly found the way?

(4) One of the most important parts of spiritual life is prayer. A glance at the teaching of the French Oratorians[4] and the Russian Starzians[5] relating to prayer shows how little we know about the right attitude. We pray consciously, pensively, actively. The inner prayer which is atmosphere, harbored in divine truth, is passive. The Self induces the attitude of soul which is the premise for internal prayer. This passivity is different from quietism: it is alert recollection on the border of the divine sea so that the waves of the supernatural constantly lap around and bathe it. Ancient teachings on prayer and modern depth psychology converge.

(5) The Self is connected with another element which is secretly encapsuled in the core of the person, the *conscience*. Self-realization for the Christian equals practical formation of conscience. Each conditions and influences the other. This is a basic fact of moral psychology. Demands of morality and of the life of the soul encounter and complement each other in self-realization, like theory and practice. As a result, there is a more profound awareness of, and refined use of, the concepts of Sin and Guilt, temptation and intention, and so forth. Formation of conscience thus no longer consists of one-sided lectures

---

[4] Cf. Henri Brémond, *Das wesentliche Gebet* (Regensburg, 1939).

[5] Cf. Igor Smolitsch, *Leben und Lehre der Starzen* (Vienna, 1936).

and adoption of moral ground rules, of constantly
repeated orientation accordingly, with a psychological
annex on temperament, character, influence of education, and environment. True—it is all this, but also
much more. Beyond this, formation of conscience
consists in showing the individual layers of the soul
how to conform with the demands of morality, in
explaining and working out the detours and byways
so as to enable the Christian in the world to live a
Christian life. Under this aspect, formation of conscience is a Christian education molding an independent man, who, having found himself and become
entirely himself, can stand before God in free and
responsible decision and listen to the call of God in
all questions of ethics with every fibre of his being.

(6) Just as the analyst presents the greatest
problem in psychotherapy, so does the priest in the
care of souls. The psychotherapeutic schools insist
that their students undergo a training analysis by an
established and well-regarded psychotherapist. The
beginner is forced to face up to himself, he is led to
himself and hardened against deception of his own
projection, so that he will be able to help objectively.
In the relationship between analyst and student are
echoes of other relationships that have always played
an important part in Christian life: master-disciple,
novice master-novice, confessor-penitent. Priesthood
demands from man a high degree of cultivated and
discerning humanity. Even though the education of
priests nowadays can be termed high-level compared
to that of other epochs of church history, much can
be expected from the application of depth psychology
to the formation of the younger generation of priests.
The pastoral function of the priest as shepherd will

thus be enriched, since he will be able to trace not only the sin but the error in the soul and bring the erring back through knowledge of its depth. His own humanity, too, must be worked out in the direction of self-realization if he, as a priest, is expected to create the same atmosphere which surrounded Jesus when the sinners thronged to Him. If education in seminaries will concern itself with depth psychology, it will radiate, and the relationship of master-disciple or novice-master-novice will develop freely and without being forced, without application of rules, coming from the inside. The young theologian actually searches for a master in the full sense of the word. A professor teaches, a superior is concerned with the smooth ordering of things, but a master forms men and imparts spiritual life. Depth psychology thus is effective by influencing the formation of priests indirectly by means of the personality of the educator. Lectures on depth psychology and psychotherapy are only secondary means in the practical formation of the seminarians. The material has to be chosen very carefully: depth psychology requires more maturity than is usually found at 24, the usual age for priest's ordination. Instruction of priests in depth psychology should begin only after a few years of practice.

Judging from the variety of tasks and the wide range demanded, it is clear that a priest's occupation with depth psychology does not create a clever psychologist, but that more is at stake here: his *humanitas christiana*. It should be a distinctive mark of the priest. Only as a consecrated man and human being can he avoid the pitfalls of bureaucracy and empty activism. He matures into a "father" who imparts life.

(7) As a precious by-product of psychotherapy,

we might expect a textbook on psychic sicknesses. Such a book should contain the presentation of the most prevalent forms of neuroses as well as an easy-to-follow, practical guide for the cure of light cases. Just as every physician has a "Handbook of Minor Surgery" and has to know something about the possibilities of major surgery so that he can refer the patient to a specialist, so there is need for a "Handbook of Minor Psychotherapy" for the pastor. The greater possibilities for major psychotherapy must be sketched in so that he is able to call in a specialist where necessary, be he a professional psychotherapist or a priest with psychotherapeutic training. Much help and comfort for psychic trouble could be achieved in this way; the forum of the Sacrament of Penance, however, would be freed of cases erroneously considered guilty.

IV

In conclusion, it seems to be clear that more is at stake in the development of depth psychology for spiritual guidance than just psychology, which has been surpassed by the fruition of Christian life. Spiritual guidance does not "psychologize," but opens layers of being for Christianization. The new knowledge of the life of the soul enables the pastor to guide his faithful towards a development of their being and thus prepares the soul for the spiritual growth of "another Christ." To quote Theodore Müncker, "Self-development is the ontic foundation for Christ-development." Both, self-realization and Christ-realization, are interdependent. Human endeavor in spiritual guidance and the effects of grace unite in the aim "to become conformed to the image of his Son" (Rom. 8:29).

3:   PASTORAL CARE
CALLS THE PERSON

This theme is dynamically formulated. The act of calling is a motion which will cause a countermotion. Pastoral care, too, is a call which expects an answer. This call is of such a nature that not only intellect and will, but also the emotions, can react. Yet these are only partial answers. Pastoral care addresses itself to the carrier of all this, to the center of man, to his person.

The person is called upon: this is made possible by means of the dynamic structure of the call. Whatever is existent within man as personally activated reality—that is, its static foundation—is induced into the act by the call from without, and thus by the call of the educator, the psychotherapist, and the pastor.

Educating, therefore, means not only aiding in the development of personal gifts, but also calling forth the dynamics of the person. He who educates aids the maturing of the person.

Healing in psychotherapy is not only repairing of the psychic apparatus, but also, and even more so, a confrontation between the healing call of the psychotherapist and the imprisoned or distorted core of the patient's person.

Pastoral care does not seek to heal but to bring salvation. It is not so much concerned with transmitting knowledge that leads to pious emotions and practices, but rather with confronting the human person

with the person of God through the call to faith, and
to help him to full actuation in this call-and-reply
event.

The character of this call in education, psychotherapy, and pastoral care should be a counterweight
to the tendency of our time which, because of its mass
tendency and its employment of mass communication,
is hostile to the person. Increasing rationalization has
the effect of suction. More and more fields of human
endeavor lie within this phase of transition which
apparently is necessary, and in which so much is
facilitated for us by norm and machine. As little as
we can avoid this development—which would represent flight from reality, taboo in psychotherapy as
well as in the proclamation of the gospel—we still
have to find a means of facing it, along with its bur-
densome side-effects. This certainly cannot take place
in the dimension in which quantity, abundance and
mass are sovereign, that is, through an even greater
supply of knowledge and the noteworthy. The technical culture of our time produces so many assertions
that the over-all culture is beginning to resemble
nothing more than a bundle of answers—what questions they answer no one knows. But the questioner
within man, the one who seeks answers not only because they interest him but because he needs them,
and who desperately defends himself against the
soporific oversupply of the answer-peddlers—this
questioner constitutes the psychic seat which is not
found in the dimensions of breadth or length, but
rather within the dimension of depth, or even better,
in the inner being, in that openness that is found in
the dimensions of the personal. It may be necessary to
send streams into this territory to nourish and awaken

it so that the seed can mature for the whole of life.

In the twofold relationship of educator and student, of psychotherapist and patient, of pastor and man, all the aspects of this problem of danger and rescue are focused as rays under a sun glass. All the problems, in psychotherapy as well as in pastoral care, will be acutely evident under the signs of need and help: the individual in himself, his relation to sex, his relation to the community, and his relation to the cosmos. In these four sensitive points—sensitive for psychotherapy as well as for pastoral care—the personal character of a call for pastoral care in our times will be demonstrated.

I

One of the great needs driving patients into the consulting room of the psychotherapist is the feeling of insecurity; the absence of security is felt, not so much from the outside but rather from the inside, within a man. Such people do not like to be alone with themselves; they are warring with themselves, split within themselves, a burden to themselves. It is well known that the cause for this rootlessness is often to be found in the childhood of the patient, and that healing consists in a retracing of the whole development—the reconciliation with himself as ultimate goal. The individual should find his own, his existential, authenticity so that he can take root within himself and, based on his own foundations, can attain the significance and the value of his personal existence. "I have a right to exist," say the basic energies of the psyche; and we could speak of the right to existence of everybody else. The fact that one person can find the way to self-realization makes it possible for him to confront a partner, that is, to enter into a personal relationship. This is healing work which aims directly at the actualization of the person. Self-realization is a condition for personal relationship.

How does pastoral care influence the self-realization of those seeking help from it? This is a very sensitive and painful question, because the priest—clad in the cloth of solemnity and oppressive power—can disturb man in his self-realization and even drive him into uncertainty and insecurity. Thus a healthy feeling of one's own worth can be distorted into guilt feelings, insecurity and consciousness of sin before the threatening God. Before God, man is a nothing, a sinner only. Apart from the fact that pastoral works in this sense are not effective any more except, perhaps, with neurotics, we must ask ourselves how this negative side of pastoral care will influence man's concept of the whole structure of Christian faith. Here we may say that words like guilt and penance express indeed a basic tenet of the Christian concept and must bear marks of a sound emphasis in preaching, but such an assertion simply means that we have barely reached the threshold. On the inside there is another message to be heard. God is not only interested in each individual, but He also wants to address him, talk to him, and engage him as a partner in a dialogue. In front of the God of the gospel, man is *not* a nothingness but is recognized as an individual on his own merits; he is regarded as a beloved, individual creature. Remission of sin and forgiveness is not the only topic in the dialogue between God and man and is favored neither from man's side nor from God's. According to the model for the Christian relationship to God, that is, the relationship of Christ and His disciples, we may assume that God takes man seriously as His partner and that man, sharply delineated, has a right to existence in front of God, even as a creature. This pastoral care, if understood rightly, calls upon the faithful to bring into play their right to existence vis à vis God, and thus fit themselves to be partners. It encourages man to open up towards God, to enter into a personal relationship with God and—to speak in the language of the New Testament—enter into the new covenant. To fulfill this personal attitude towards God is the task of personal pastoral care.

II

In psychotherapy many people learn for the first time to think and speak in parables and symbols. During dream-analysis patient and analyst often talk on two different levels and yet they understand each other despite the constant interchange of outside actuality and veiled symbols. What is experienced here is the capability for the symbol, something which the mass has lost but which the individual has to relearn, even outside psychotherapy. The symbol veils; but in its transparency and unity it hints at the significance of what is hidden. The symbol is transparent: the invisible significance becomes visible, tangible, even audible. It sparkles in the symbol, it illuminates it as if it were present. In the genuine symbol the invisible can be experienced as reality.

The knowledge that all things in this world can be transparent has the effect of a new discovery in man, who comes from a world of unequivocal push-buttons, robots, file cards, and the similarly unequivocal abbreviations of our technical language. The capability for symbols infuses man with a new relationship to the surrounding world. Fire, water, light, stone,

plant, and animal will become transparent for the
spiritual, so that the spiritual and the material do not
fall apart like things that have nothing in common. By
the same token the spiritual is conceptualized ma-
terially. The next step would be that one's own body
will be experienced and realized in its transparency.
Thus the rejecting, compulsive motion of the hand
of a neurotic patient can, during treatment, become
liberated into a consciously expressed gesture. Incor-
poration—"becoming flesh" of the psyche—makes
man free.

Now man is prepared not only to use another man
but to really *see* him, because the other confronts
him bodily. Who he is, is symbolized in the body. In
order to read this symbol for the person of the other,
experience in transparence is necessary. Eyes, ears, and
hands are capable of expressing symbols, and necessary for seeing not only the body of the other but
also the "becoming flesh" of the other person, as
well as to open up, in curious resonance, for the
personal call. Person is resonant to person. Not only
outside contact, such as occurs in a business transac-
tion, but encounter on the personal level is becoming
possible.

This encounter with symbols can come to its full
blossoming in love. When two young people are in
love—insofar as they are aware of their chances, and
insofar as the tension between Eros and sex is not dissolved prematurely by activation of the sexual—the
body and face of the other are illuminated by transparency, and one has such a power of call for the
other that that person opens up and the individualis-
tic attitude, the loneliness, come off like wrappings.
The person learns that he is created for *dialogue,* and

the miracle of dignified human belonging is experienced anew. "Becoming flesh" is a step in the actualization of the person.

This "becoming flesh" is carried on in pastoral care through the principle of incarnation. To incarnate means to become flesh—"The word has become flesh" (John 1:14), as we usually translate it. Christ, the only begotten Son of God, is "the true likeness of the God we cannot see" (Col. 1:15). He is veil and revelation at the same time—incarnation of God and transparent for the divine manner of being and living: "Whoever has seen me, has seen the Father" (John 14:9). The Christmas Preface says: ". . . and through him whom we recognize as God made visible may we be caught up into a love of things unseen." In pastoral care the proclamation is modeled after the same way in which the incarnation of the divine takes place in the secular: it entrusts the transparence of all things, starting with the word, to the actions of the liturgy.

The symbolic actions of the liturgy veil the realities of God while at the same time, through their comprehensibility, they reveal His presence in the mystery. Thus, the true Christian mystery-celebration can become the personal encounter with God—as long as we have learned to see the spiritual in incarnation. In celebrating the liturgy, man can break through immanence and conquer the false dimensions of his technical world; through his ability to think in symbols he can be transported, as by wings, to comprehend transparency. Every material thing in the liturgy becomes transparent, a bearer of the supernatural, the spiritual; and in the Sacrament of the Eucharist it becomes a bearer even for the personal presence of the Lord. It is not just a coincidence that Christians who undergo psychotherapy become open toward symbols and thus toward the liturgy. What they need to work out through analysis shows—as if under a microscope—what each of us would need' individually. Symbol, transparency, "becoming flesh," incarnation, liturgy—all these are necessary steps which can lead to the dimension of the personal.

In the word of preaching—the proclaimed word— the law of incarnation is fulfilled when the "shape of the proclamation" is felt. The word links speaker and listener. The word of preaching elevates them to the plane of event—messenger, message, receiver—and insofar as the preacher becomes a messenger—that is, does not preach his own word but through faith realizes his word as the witnessing word—his activity can become transparent for the relationship: God addresses man, calls for and expects an answer from man. The person of God encounters the human person in the event of the proclamation.

III

Weakness in maintaining contacts has become so prevalent in present-day society that it exceeds mere individual inhibition and, instead, suggests a symptom of deeper damage. It cannot be repaired by means of technical organization, by providing occasions to meet in common or for amusement. To be alone in the midst of a crowd increases isolation, and the lack of true community engenders a need which desperately cries for the help of "therapeutic communication." The straw grasped in gratefulness—the acceptance into the sheltering atmosphere of the therapist—is only a guide line, an exercise-ground, and an exchange point in the journey to the depths of human existence where we can find the common grounds on which we all stand. This, however, can happen only when the therapist does not content himself with the technical aspect of his treatment, but engages himself in the therapeutic dialogue and takes a stand. If person is resonant to person, only such a therapist will be able to lead the patient needing help from the individual shallows to the depths of common human existence wherein a structural element of the human person can be experienced—the "being-created," the creatureliness. The human person in contrast to the divine infinite person has a beginning; it is created, it is creature, and this is the element which must come to the fore in personal life. If it were experienced, it would constitute a common ground where people are equal and could meet each other as human brother and human sister. Whether expressed in words or not, there would be a situation in a really deep-searching analysis when the patient might formulate a question similar to this: "What are our chances—yours as the therapist, and mine as the patient—in the world?" This is a question probing for the religious significance of life. Only real inner anguish leads to such a question, which distresses—not emotionally but existentially. Real help would be provided in this case only if the therapist would indicate that he and the patient are standing on the same ground and that he, too, is constantly pondering the question of what chance he himself and all of us together have in this world. Community is experienced in sober, naked truth. Creatureliness is a healthy and healing fact, because it is comprehensive truth. He who rises to the surface after diving into the depth—back to the

human community—can look upon it differently. He
has gained the inner ability to experience it from a
common basis. He has returned from isolation and is
able to "take his place in line" without feeling de-
graded. He has realized within himself the saving
dimension, the creaturely element of the person. He
is able to insert himself into the group of those
who help because he himself has become able to
communicate—not technically, organization-wise, but
existentially or personally.

This is exactly the point at which pastoral care
begins; it is done less from the moral call of love of
neighbor, but from much deeper, more comprehensive
motives that are pregnant with authenticity. It knows
not only the beginning but also the chances for the
future and can interpret the present as the "between-
time"—the *tempus medium* of St. Augustine. These
are the three great lines of salvation history, the
teaching of the three eons, the median of which is
our time and has to be seen in relativity to the first
eon, the stage of paradise, and the third eon, the kingdom of God after the second coming of the Lord. The
creature's existential question about "his chance in
the world" is absorbed by pastoral care and is formulated in concrete form, through theology, as the question for "salvation or perdition" of mankind in
which the individual participates. The experience of
creatureliness flows into the experience of the common need of salvation. The answer of salvation history
in the eon theory inserts the individual into the community of man and addresses him in this community.
Salvation no longer means simply a personal being
accepted by God but a liberation of mankind from
the condition of the second eon to the condition of

the third, the transposition of the "between-time" into the Kingdom of God which comprises God and mankind. Christianity is not just "a private, mystical adventure but also a cosmic one," as Hans Urs von Balthasar says. In Christian faith creatureliness is pressed into realization as one structural element of the person.

IV

The words of Ernst Jünger that "God must be conceptualized anew"[1] characterizes the religious problems not only of many patients in psychotherapy but of many people in general. One does not want to get involved in abysmally theoretical discussions of a new theology. But the pressing desire at the conclusion of psychotherapy, and also in the case of all those who have awakened to their humanness, is the question of how the relationship to God can be realized. The impression is given that the old formulas have lost their cogency and that religious restlessness is seeking new ones.

Several different developments underlie this great religious commotion. We do not propose to examine here how much the more or less conscious disappointment with the philosophical answers of the nineteenth century has had to do with this. Add to this the conquest of space made possible only through men's technical progress, but which, despite its success, tends to depersonalize man by depriving him of his humanity. Where in space can man find God—or, rather, where is the door which would lead to Him? Such questions indicate, ever more and more clearly, that the personal plane is the only escape from the

---

[1] *Strahlungen* (Tübingen, 1949), p. 25f.

massification and collectivation that exists even in the religious sphere.

The religious restlessness which belongs with the "depth structure of the psychic base" (Lotz) knocks at the door of transcendence. But in contrast to earlier times it is no longer satisfied with hints at the absolute Being, or a divine sense of the whole of the world. The transcendence movement of today is concretized and becomes more outspoken in its longing; it does not seek the general Divine but holds that transcendence can be proved only in the personal sphere, and anticipates the encounter with the divine person. Just as corporeal thirst indicates the presence of water, so religious longing, which is constantly becoming clearer, indicates divine encounter with God as a person. This religious thirst will become more pronounced as soon as the shock of recognition has penetrated our consciousness—recognition that for the first time in history not only the things fashioned by man have left the globe and gone out into space but also man himself, in the flesh, with whom, as the physicists explain, not even a common link of time unites us. The specter of homelessness and complete disorientation touches the foundation of our world-consciousness with an icy finger. At the present time, this shock is still concealed by the global conflict of men divided among themselves. This is a shock with religious consequences, similar to the one in Columbus' time when it was realized that the earth was a globe and that distance leads back to the point of departure, proving that it too was imprisoned in itself. Then, too, religious concepts were shaken by an internal earthquake which contributed to the destruction of the world-feeling of the Middle Ages.

The question of transcendence, the beyond, of what and who is beyond the threshold, can no longer be satisfyingly answered with philosophical answers. It needs to be posited anew; it demands precise answers. How can it be demonstrated that the personal dimension is able to live beyond the dimensions of space and time? *That* is something one would like to realize.

In this sense, pastoral care is confronted with the task of creating "a new concept of God," one that will effect the realization of this transcendental movement in an enlarged view of the world. It can do so by a precise reference to the forty days after Easter during the lifetime of Jesus. Here a man proves that it is possible in the body—in the transfigured state of the human body—to pass the threshold of transcendence everywhere and at any time. Sacred Scripture reports eleven apparitions. He who does not know this person of Jesus Christ should endeavor to meet it; he will then realize the importance of these reports of apparitions. The threshold of transcendence —the threshold of death—can be passed, and passed by man; and since the Ascension, not only on the globe but wherever man is, even in space. With this, the cosmos becomes spiritually "passable" for him for whom the person of Christ in faith has become the "way" and the "door."

Theologically, this precise reasoning is guaranteed by the realization of the humanity of Christ—of the resurrected Christ, too, as the one who passed the threshold. In pastoral care, the picture of Jesus has moved into new focus: it is not so much a picture of the regal Christ, the pantocrator of Christian antiquity, who helps us realize our faith in our time, or the exalted man of sorrows of the Middle Ages, nor the

Jesus of inwardness of modern times, but the resurrected Jesus in the flesh—Christ who appeared in the flesh, ascended to heaven and is enthroned there, who is our pledge that the person is able to live in the beyond. This means, theologically speaking, the "complete humanization of the divine" (Urs von Balthasar). "God is today experienced under the aspect of the human" (Alfons Rosenberg). Theology might regard this as a mere act of removing dust from a precious old piece of furniture; but it is not a question of the content of speculative theology but of realization of the religious sense in the space age—to enter into which and to subsist in which is our task in the midst of the polarity of mass and person.

The encounter with the divine person of the man Jesus Christ, to which pastoral care is directed, is the highest call which can be issued to a human person. It is enclosed in human words and liturgical acts, like symbols. Our answer presupposes individuality, which receives through the experience of creatureliness its just measure in the face of the divine person. The tie with Christ in faith stretches beyond the threshold of transcendence in an intensive actuation of personal life. Here may lie the possibility of passing the test, not only of the adventure of our society but also, in a human way, of the space age.

4: CHARACTERISTICS OF RELIGIOUS LIFE TODAY

The fundamental posture of religious life is two-fold: God calls—man listens. Consequently, the exposition of religious life in our times can be classified in two parts: the specific characteristics of God's call in the present, concerning which theology is searching for clarity; and the characteristics of man as listener and respondent of today. Anthropology is searching for insights and answers which should help attain a better understanding and greater ability to help those who are entrusted to us.

I

God has spoken emphatically on two occasions—in creation and in Revelation. The world as creation is God's call even though it has changed rapidly in the course of its development. It is through it that God addresses man. And in the Bible we have God's Revelation, even though we read it with different eyes in our present age—it remains God's word. That these changes are related to each other like connecting tubes indicates the specific religious trait of our times: in theological endeavor the main stress is no longer on the questions of how "man can attain salvation," or how he can arrive at his own justification before God, or how he can enter heaven. All these represent knowledge about and striving for the individual way to salvation, in which the question of good and evil, of sin and absolution, plays the main part. Each time it is the question of an individual relationship to God, of an internal religious experience which does not necessarily find external expression but may remain within the inner space, opening up all the possibilities of inner (inward) spirituality, but lying exposed at the same time to the dangers of religious narcissism. These questions remain actual; they have not been abolished or replaced; they are not secondary but remain a permanent religious concern.

But a new kind of call, caused by the changing world picture, has gone forth from God to the man who is seriously working on his own salvation. It disturbs the quiet of man immersed in his religiosity and causes him to open his eyes and confront the new religious reality. The world of man is drifting toward a new stage, not only through the population explosion and the closing of the gap between the various nations that has resulted from technical progress, but, above all, through political constellations, which have divided mankind into a few power blocs that are responsible for the choice between destruction of the earth or cooperation. The perils connected with this penetrate our emotions like the smell of fire and, as a consequence, alter religious questions. It is no longer only concern with my own salvation that counts. I am on a ship, the ship of humanity, whose passengers are scanning the horizon with great hope. Theologically speaking, this means that my own way of salvation is a part of that way of salvation for mankind which theology calls salvation history. The individual is inserted into the comprehensive multitude, just as the passenger, who, though he leads an individual life aboard ship, belongs to the ship's complement on its voyage. Salvation history, the present great topic of theology, is the movement in which personal striving is included. This means a change in the structure of modern man's experience, an increase of breadth and depth, a greater burden but also a clearer meaning against which the human psyche may react defensively, since strange religious connections have a disquieting effect. However, the contrary may also occur: a feeling of thankfulness for the religious affirmation of the global concept may take over.

The shift of accent from the individual way of salvation to collective salvation history is like the shifting to a new, additional register on an organ. The principal stress is no longer on the individual but on the common denominator. Not only the individual's religion is important but the fate of the whole community, as well. The family of man becomes transparent to God's designs. Not only my own relations with good and evil pass sentence on me, but the salvation or perdition of the world. While etiology, namely, the teaching for perdition, for restitution in redemption—in brief, teachings about the past—has thus far pre-empted most of the gospel interpretations, eschatology—the teachings about the "last things" toward which the ship of mankind is sailing—has been neglected. But eschatology is now moving into the foreground. This has its effect in Catholic concerns, even to the point of changing the image of Christ, insofar as it is not so much the Savior of Souls who is considered religiously effective as the risen Christ—He who has passed through the cross to the beyond and came back, the Lord of the Return.

The great value of this concept of the future will gradually attain recognition in psychic experience in comparison to that of the past. The frozen static of religiosity will be thawed and will pave the way for a dynamic switch in orientation toward a future that, unlike the past, is open. The streams of psychic energy are attracted by the future.

In summing up, we can see the result of all this to be a change in direction of religious feeling from the inner to the outer world. This religious feeling confronts the realities of the outside world in a new way. One might characterize the significance of religious life in our day as a breakthrough, in space and time, to outside reality—as a new relationship to the world.

A second characteristic of religious life today comprises the process of mass civilization. The opening of all spiritual spheres to the masses by the technical means of radio, television, and film has a negative side-effect: while public opinion is raised to unheard-of effectiveness, because the masses respond with great sensitivity this means more dependence. In the measure that a person, or many people, participate in public opinion, they live and think and feel as a mass. The houses of their souls are inhabited by cliché opinions and less and less by their own responsible convictions. It is a phenomenon perceived more and more that in many spheres of life a man does not live but is lived; yet the religious life shows a countertendency. Public opinion reacts negatively to everything religious and, if it has to face it, labels it as custom or comparative religious science. The true religious life, however, is beginning to retreat from this idea of custom and is, sometimes secretly, sometimes openly, in opposition to the masses. Therefore, religious life finds itself more in a situation of conflict than of habit, and leads the religious person into isolation. The individual splits off the mass not as a matter of course but as a consequence of pressure and counterpressure. If a person wants to lead a religious life, he puts himself in a position of contradiction to the over-all opinion, is isolated, and is thus pressured into a decision. This is the second characteristic of religious life: it is more and more tied to conscious decision. The decisive factor in the psyche is evoked and is religiously obligated. To say "No" to religious life does not bring in its wake the same disadvantages as once upon a time when it meant becoming a social outcast. But if man decides for religion, it is patently a truly religious decision made in full freedom. The characteristic of decision is thus emphasized in the religious life of today. Modern religion is connected with decision, not only with maturing, growing, and becoming from the inside but also with a conscious position in relation to the outside world. This is again a confrontation with outside reality and it forces us to question its effect on the psyche.

A third characteristic of religious life today will have to be mentioned with certain restrictions, inasmuch as it occurs only sporadically in Protestantism, passes as a general and clear sign of religious life in the Catholic Church, and is often considered with longing outside the Church. It is the rediscovery of the mystery celebration. The liturgical renewal which has taken place in the last half-century was not instituted, but is the expression of a world-wide movement among men. Here they are touching upon a reality in the liturgical mystery. We can only say that this reality is independent and different from the powers of consciousness in the psyche and from the unconscious powers, as well as of the core of the psyche, the self. We can say that consciousness recognizes its significance clearly and searches after it; that the unconscious mysteriously subordinates itself to the mystery celebration; and that this reality can be grasped when the self opens toward it in personal encounter. Thus the experience of the mystery celebration can be a religious sign of our times serving as call and answer in the opening-up toward outside reality.

All three characteristics—the concern with the world, the character of decision, and the mystery celebration—point in the same direction, toward a break-through to outward reality. In religious life they underline the stress on relationship with the outside world in contrast to the inner-directed process of integration, and they even subordinate the integration of the psyche to this religious relationship with the outside. By this slow conversion from the introverted character of religious life, our religious life of the present seems to veer toward an extrovert tendency. The second part of this article will be concerned with the effects of this change of direction towards the outer world and will explain how the three characteristics are mirrored in today's life.

II

If concern with the world dominates our religious life, religion emerges from the shell of a "thingless" life. Previously the things of the world and the things of religion were separated. One retired from the activities of the world into the inner space, to meditation and contemplation, and called this abiding in the inner spaces of the psyche the religious life. This inward direction was held to be the pledge of con

nection with the divine, so that this space was first
filled by pictures and motivations from holy books, to
which the depth of the psyche responded, until the
to-and-fro movements were succeeded by stillness in
which the presence of the mysterious could be felt.
This way to the innermost reality is "thingless"; it is
"devotion without word"; and from this evolved a
"world without devotion."[1] Seen religiously, the world
often is nothing but a waiting room for life after
death, or an examination hall where test has to be
passed for entrance into the beyond. Worldly activity
and religion are separated, the world itself lacking a
religious relationship, at best offering only an attempt
at such. Religious life is a retreat into the cloisters
of the soul where the psychic dialogue with God can
take place.

When we now assert in the face of this that the
relationship to the world has to be inserted into the
psychic process—and this in a dominating way—a
shifting of values has to take place in the psychic
sphere so that more emphasis is placed on the conscious in comparison to the unconscious, outer space
as confronted with inner, so that the scales are once
more weighted on the side of rational powers. The
consciously religious interest in the divine plan demands its place at the side of the religious dialogue
in the wings. The shift of interest from the individual
way of salvation to collective salvation history confronts the "enjoyed stillness and connection with the
mysterious"—the familiar dialogue with the Savior
of souls—with the new religious content of the con-

---

[1] Cf. H. J. Schulz, *Frömmigkeit in einer weltlichen
Welt* (Olten, 1962).

scious, and it demands that a position be taken. Activity is no longer confined to the psychic enclosed space. Religious energy flows into conscious connection with the plan of salvation, and plan is sometimes experienced as a relative weakening of the inner world of wonder. Psychologically speaking, one might say that modern religious life is becoming psychologically thinner, but that a soberer and clearer consciousness is emerging. The relationship to the world demands that retreat to the inmost recesses be coupled with clear knowledge of the outside world, the knowledge of time and space in a certain phase of the current of salvation history. Religious life is connected with salvation history, is localized in it, and is historically determined. This relationship is by itself religiously significant. Not only is there devotion in the midst of the world, but the being-in-the-world process is itself religious. Religious life breaks through to the outside reality.

What happens within the psyche when the second symbol of our days, the character of decision, dominates habitual tradition and the purely inner-psychic development and occurrences? Decision determines for one side against the other. To decide against an environment presupposes a distance, isolates and circumscribes, and makes us conscious of being confined to the state of an individual. Pressure from the outside increases, which changes the consciousness in some strange way as if the conscious were receiving a new dimension, or as if a door would open behind it into a new space where somebody is staying who would make the decisions and take the responsibility for them. Thus a third instance of the psyche enters into religious life, which not only comprises and unites the conscious and the unconscious, which not only merely exists and breathes but which opens its eyes and becomes something—the core of my individuality, I myself, the Self, or, in philosophical parlance, the persona.

The character of decision colors the self with a religious tint, calling it, awakening it, or, again in philosophical parlance, actuating the persona. Man confronts himself, takes hold of himself, stands here as a whole, "exists." This is a sober happening and a sober experience, certainly not the result of a religious exuberance, nor of any wave of piety, but rather an activity which surveys the world of religious emotions and symbols and also looks beyond it.

This looking-beyond means not only decision against, but decision for something or somebody as well. This represents the focus of modern anthropological research.[2] The self or persona makes possible contact with the outside world not only in the way of intellectual theories and agreements and not only in emotional implications, but as an encounter as well. This encounter takes place not only with the mysterious character of the world in numinous experience but also with persons. And it is here that the true Christian way is initiated: in the encounter with the person of the messenger of God under the form of His own Son, or of His delegate, the priest. Religious decision, then, means not only decision for the numinous character of the mystery of the world—which already represents a break-through from the inner psychic space to the outer reality—but decision

---

[2] Cf., for example, Theoderich Kampmann, *Erziehung und Glaube* (Munich, 1961).

for a person, who confronts me independently from myself, with a sober hardness and severity for decision that only an outer reality is able to exert. Here religious experience becomes belief in somebody. In this encounter the actual density of a person—the heightened intensity of life in the self—is experienced.[3] The psychic act of integration retroactively receives a final increase by means of the highest relationship, that of contact with a divine person. In the Christian sphere we are, therefore, accustomed to speak of personalization of faith. One might universalize this by saying that the character of decision in religious life pushes religious experience toward personalization. Religious education is therefore directed toward the categories of personal space.

The third and last-mentioned symbol of our times was seen in the search for experience in the mysteries, or Catholically speaking, in the celebration of the liturgy. The rejection of and the timidity before the mystery celebration comes from an intellectual objection. As a grownup, one does not want to fall back to the level of magic, does not want to succumb to projections, that is, to concretizations¯ of psychically unconscious maturing processes. But this reservation is often coupled with a desire, expressed frequently in friendly envy, to participate in the mysterious reality of the mystery celebration as it is celebrated in the Catholic Church, because one is "fed up" with solely inner-psychic motives. Does man as *homo religiosus,* in spite of all rationalism, want to realize

---

[3] Cf. also Bollnow, *Existenzphilosophie und Pädagogik* (Stuttgart, 1959); Guardini-Bollnow, *Begegnung und Bildung* (Würzburg, 1956).

and concretize in an outward direction? How is this possible without slipping back into the mythical unconscious? How should the highly conscious man of today celebrate mysteries? What is expressed in this new world-wide desire for mysteries? What changes take place in religious life when mysteries are celebrated?

Mysteries are constructed of human and divine realities separated by a dividing line, death, or the deadly, the death zone. In the mystery we try to pass over the threshold and to establish contact between the two partners so that the two realities may touch each other. Religious spiritualism wants to separate this confrontation from outside reality, and to work it out spiritually in individual, knowing absorption into the "chambers of the soul." But this means isolation within the inner psychic space. It is the experience of depth psychology, however, that a human being tries to express itself in the body as well as in thought, so that the "sacred meal," for instance, not only means symbol and motive for the integration of sacred and profane parts of the soul but is a genuine model for the hospitality of God, at whose table man wants to seat himself and to see God seat Himself opposite him. Such a happening would correspond to the nature of man and be a real mystery celebration. Let us cite an example of what we mean.

The new regulations for the Holy Week rites place a curious and sensible rite at the center of the Good Friday services, the veneration of the cross. During a chant which is repeated three times a large cross is unveiled: first the right arm, then the left arm, and in the end the corpus of the crucified—for contemplation and identification of the cross as a symbol of redemption. Then the people are called to the actual veneration. They approach the altar singly and kneel before the cross symbol, inclining their heads and then either touching with their hand or kissing with their lips the figure on the cross. If this is meant to be more than just a pious ceremony, the event of venerating the cross needs to be explained.

The cross is a sign of victory, of victory over death. He who hangs from the cross before us died in a very peculiar manner. Voluntarily, knowingly, He yielded up His spirit with a loud cry (Mark 15:27), penetrating the death-happenings, penetrating the death zone with His human and divine power—in short, overcoming death. We all need such death strength. And when we approach the cross as the symbol of this dying, and while we kneel before it and bow our heads or touch it, we pray that Jesus' dying powers will be ours. Can an enlightened Catholic do so following that kind of explanation? The mystery celebration demands that he overcome his confinement to the inner space and act. Thus it can happen that his faithful observing, knowing and stating becomes acting, and that he experiences religion as a whole man by discarding his own fragmentation. It seems to be the secret longing of people in the Church and its forecourts to be able to achieve this action. This means that religious experience today is searching for the form, the mode, in which human life would like to fulfill itself, which means expression with soul and body, expression in the wholeness.

To sum up the present state of knowledge, the duties this knowledge imposes on pastoral care are as follows:

The relationship of religious life to the world places it in a new relation to time and space and demands the break through the inner sphere of the psyche. The demand on pastors is for the proclamation of the gospel as salvation history.

The character of decision in religious life evokes the instance through which a contact with the outside world can be realized, the persona. The demand on pastors is for a personalization of Christianity.

The mystery celebration, finally, leads religious experience to fulfillment, in which man learns to live in the wholeness of his being with respect to God. The demand on pastors is for a true, authentic and sensible celebration of the mysteries in the liturgy.

5:

PSYCHOTHERAPY
AND CONFESSION

Let us start with a quote from Kierkegaard's Introduction to *Sickness Unto Death:* "All Christian presentation must be like the attitude of the physician at a sickbed." All Christian teaching, including talk about confession, is similar to the physician's attitude at the sick bed. By this, Kierkegaard does not mean, of course, the sick bed in clinic or hospital, or the situation in the consulting room of the psychotherapist, but the sick bed of mankind. Revelation says that man is "sick," with guilt and penance, but this sickness lies in another sphere than the sickness of the body or the psyche, which can be cured by the physician or the psychotherapist. In this regard there is a basic difference between physician and priest, between penitent and patient, between confession and psychotherapy.[1] This difference is significant for our times because there is danger of overlapping at the borderlines, which is harmful for both and does not aid cooperation. We shall therefore stress here precisely

---

[1] In our context psychotherapy is understood as: Psychoanalysis of Sigmund Freud; Individual psychology of Alfred Adler; Analytical psychology of C. G. Jung; Existential analysis of Medard Boss, Ernst Michel, von Gebstattel and others. Andreas Snoek, in his book *Confession and Psychoanalysis* (Frankfurt, 1958), argues only in the field of Freudian psychoanalysis, which constitutes a limitation of this otherwise excellent work.

what is different, show the sharp delineations, and warn away from dilettante application of psychotherapeutic methods especially in the institution of confession.

The temptation to dilettantism is great. Books on psychotherapy are often written in a popular style since their subject concerns something human, that is, the psyche. It is often made to appear as if it were only through modern depth psychology—in contrast to "school psychology" or the metaphysical psychology of scholasticism—that the natural life of the psyche was discovered, not only the conscious part of the psyche but also its unconscious, the deep layers.

This is how Dr. Paul Rusch, bishop of Innsbruck, could tell the Congress of Psychotherapists in Hall in 1954 that he was constantly visited by priests who complained how little they understood about the main subject of their pastoral work, the human soul. The bishop's conclusion was not a recommendation that pastors should study psychotherapy, but that depth psychologists, out of their experience, should construct a theory for the life of the healthy man of any age, which then could be employed by pastors in the different ramifications of their activities.

But even with all these differences, there are similarities between the attitude of the physician towards patient and the priestly offices of teacher, priest, and shepherd. Some people prefer to consult a psychotherapist in their anguish because they miss the physician's attitude in the priest, and a sort of secularized care of souls ("psychagogy") is in serious competition with the priestly care of souls.

Thus, not only do we have to make a basic differentiation between psychotherapy and confession but we also have to ask ourselves where and how there is a connection between the two, once the border lines have been clearly drawn. With either institution, the important thing at stake is the human soul, though it is the sick soul with one and the guilty soul with the other.

In the following essay we shall make three confrontations between psychotherapy and confession; we shall establish three basic differences and shall ask three times what the pastor could learn from this new branch of secular knowledge. After an initial hesitancy, the Church has never taken a purely negative attitude towards new scientific discoveries.

The guide lines which we shall follow here in this series of comparisons will be those of "need and help." In either case, man in need of help turns to the specialist, the big difference being that one sinks into the upholstered easy-chair in the consultation room of the psychotherapist while the other kneels down on the hard kneeler of the confessional. In either case, the universal, anthropological human condition of "need and help" is given. We shall compare:

(1) situation in consultation room and confessional;

(2) patient and penitent;

(3) psychotherapist and confessor.

I

CONSULTATION ROOM AND CONFESSIONAL

The patient comes to the therapist in great anguish and often as a last resort after many other attempts at being cured. His anguish is expressed in many pains which he cannot explain, such as heartpains or headaches, a feeling of the futility of life, and so on; and the psychotherapist considers all these as symptoms of something, the origin of which lies in the unconscious. His method consists in bringing to light these causes by making the patient relax and use free word-associations; by explanation of dreams and conversation as well as by the analysis of the patient's *Weltentwurf* (in the analysis of existence). The curing effect is achieved by a cleansing of the unconscious (catharsis), by recall into consciousness, by confrontation with the personal reality of the therapist (cf. Hans Trüb's *Healing through Encounter*), so that responsibility is awakened and the question of the purpose of life is asked with force, that is, put on the existential level.

The process is long and laborious and causes a complete upheaval within the patient. Analysis penetrates to his inner depth like major surgery, with all the dangers of such, and the cure often results in a complete change of personality. (It is clear that only an experienced specialist is capable of performing such treatment; any dabbling with medication by a dilettante is dangerous since the slightest overdose of the medicine administered might be poisonous.)

Therefore, a "normal" confession cannot be compared to such psychotherapeutic treatment. Nor does this comparison apply to the ordinary weekly confession; it applies only to the so-called confession of conversion, this powerful event which is the last step in the long prologue of conversion, followed by conscious and clearly formulated confession, one that clearly stands out in consciousness (since there is no unconscious and unwanted guilt in the sense of personal guilt[2]).

Guilt, therefore, is not at home in the "psychic system" with which the psychotherapist is above all concerned. Guilt exists only in the personal sphere when man, claimed by God, opposes God's will. Therefore, guilt can be contracted only in consciousness and freedom.

Psychotherapy is therefore effective only in the forecourt of confession, where man is being made capable of confronting God in freedom and responsibility. But first, man must know about God, that is, learn through Revelation how God thinks about sin and what it means to be absolved in the confessional, and that this does not come about through man's own efforts as in psychotherapy but only through God and His action. These events cannot be understood empirically because they are accessible only through a definite human attitude, that of faith.

Here is the clear cleavage between the two levels: psychotherapy is effective in the sphere of nature, and confession in that of supernature. Access to the latter is gained, not by the relaxed opening of the unconscious, transcending the conscious, but by professing a world-transcending God and answering to Him faithfully. The foremost task of the priest in the confessional is imparting of absolution; this is the sacramental reality of confession and the aim for which it was instituted; everything else that surrounds

---

[2] Karl Rahner, "Schuld und Schuldvergebung als Grenzgebiet zwischen Theologie und Psychotherapie," in *Schriften zur Theologie II,* pp. 279-297.

it—spiritual guidance and looking for grace—is of secondary importance.

The need of the patient is natural, that of the penitent supernatural. The psychotherapist's help is a natural one, the priest's a supernatural one. A combination of the two would upset the healing process and (through projection and transference) distort the view of the sacramental act.

In this way psychotherapeutical treatment and the dispensing of confession are clearly distinguished as operating on two different levels, as different as is the upholstered chair from the hard kneeler. Nor is the confessional the right place for questions which exceed the sacramental activity. The more one understands theologically and faithfully what passes between God and the sinner in this tribunal of grace which is confession, the purer he will want to keep the sacramental forum, the more he will want to protect it from all psychic events which may be stirred up when, for instance, a question penetrates to the unconscious. In this case the confessional becomes a place where the germ of confusion for the soul is spread.

Thus comparison number one, the situation in the consulting room and the confessional (viewed solely with regard to the act of treatment during consultation and the sacramental act), has shown only differences and no similarity except that in both cases a need waits for help. But psychotherapeutic help can change man so that he will find his way to the confessional, and confession sometimes smoothes the way for psychotherapeutic treatment and frees man for the cure.

II
PATIENT AND PENITENT

What the patient has to do, however, is much more than merely be present for the one- to two-hour treatment a week with the psychotherapist.[3] Between appointments he runs the gamut of feeling, from heaven to hell; his need grows worse and more insupportable and he feels dependent on the therapist, abandoned to himself, deceived and again guided; he experiences hate and love, confidence and distrust; all this he brings to the therapist who closes all the escapes and does not permit him to find a way out of this maze of inner seething. As a matter of fact, he seals him into this inner seething like an alchemist who holds his flask in the fire until the elements dissolve and combine anew in change. This alchemistic simile is more than a mere comparison: all these so-called chemical reactions are symbolic presentations of a psychic maturing process—as Jung proved —which indicate the way of change toward oneself, to the recognition of one's own truth.

In our connection it follows that the saving and healing element in neurosis must be engendered by one's own psyche. To make this development possible and to bring it to fruition is the task of psychotherapeutic art.

To illustrate this differently: it means that the psychotherapist opens all the rooms in the house of his patient's soul (the castle of the soul), gets to know all the inhabitants, tenants and subtenants with their

---

[3] In his book, *Confession and Psychoanalysis,* Andreas Snoek compares only the act of treatment and the act in the confessional.

talents and tasks, and helps them to find their place until they all come to serve the one on the throne (in the throne hall of the soul's castle), the one who could awake here and mature in the process. Without recourse to illustration, it can be said that the highest instance of the psyche is the core of the person, who through the process of treatment is destined to take over the reign of the whole, natural sphere of the psyche. In this way the patient arrives at himself, is himself, and lives his own existential truth.

In the "confession for conversion"—the only one that can furnish comparison—man's whole psychic effort is paralleled by an effort toward a development which may well last for years, and which can rightly be called a sort of spiritual guidance, "conversations of confession," outside the confessional.

Here, too, the whole of life passes in conversation, but the saving and healing element does not grow out of one's own effort and strength. The meaning of this development lies in preparing one's nature, with all its sins, for the forgiving and absolving action of God, so that what passes in the confessional is but a last step on the long road to conversion, representing not only a transformation from a sinful life to one's own truth but a transformation to the truth of God. This transformation is called conversion.

Since it is obvious that man continuously seeks to hide behind pretexts to escape the claims of God, and since it is known that the psyche erects one wing after another, that men live with such a small part of their psyche, and that whole parts of the natural sphere of the psyche are often excluded (or, to speak in an allegory, that many rooms of the house of the soul are closed and never opened)—all this makes it clear that a very thorough knowledge of psychic events and developments is extremely important. Spiritual guidance in the true meaning of the word can really profit here from the experience of psychotherapy, though it has to be separated from the life of the sick soul and worked out for the life of the healthy soul as exposed by depth psychology. Such study also makes it possible to recognize the difference between pathological and genuine confessions of guilt.

This guidance, or even a mere "accompanying" during the long-lasting development, is the problem of the confessor, as it is that of the therapist in psychotherapy. Both are supposed to be helpers-in-need, and in their personal attitude and personal power of challenge both act as sounding boards and intermediaries.

III
PSYCHOTHERAPIST AND CONFESSOR

The psychotherapist's position toward his patient is a very peculiar one: "He is neither a guide nor an interpreter nor a sage, but an 'empowerer,' "[4]—one who makes possible. Through his method, his mode of being present and being effective, he resolves resistance in the patient and thus enables the sick soul to stir, to dissolve, to grow and change in order to realize itself.

He does not judge—and the patient feels this—nor is he shocked; he is not bent on judging but on understanding. Above all, he does not weigh things in isolation but looks at them as biographical details

---

[4] Victor von Weizsäcker, *Arzt und Kranker* (Leipzig, 1941), p. 59.

and tries to understand them in context, in connection with a whole life.

The patient feels himself accepted—he has found a home. His relations to the therapist are more and more colored by projections so that a so-called transference takes place. To hold this in bounds requires all the art and experience of the therapist. During treatment he cannot efface himself. His authority is grounded in his humanity and his experience. He must become involved with the patient, but in exchange he is able to challenge him at the point where the saving element lies, in the core of his persona.

This is the attitude from which the priest can learn most for his spiritual guidance before confession, outside the confessional. However, he knows and recognizes not only symptoms but sins, and has to judge them; but two aspects, instigated by depth psychology, present themselves here:

(1) In the confessional the confessor must, of course, inquire after the formulated action, the sinful event, the sin— and, in contrast to the therapist, he must take a stand. But in the "conversation of confession" he too tries to see this as a biographical item, in connection, and in context with the whole of life. He will be able to explain the sinful deed as a symptom in the context of life.

This requires from the priest a listening attitude in conversation, which gives the penitent the feeling not of being judged and condemned but of being accepted. Even if the confessor during the sacramental act of confession is able to remain anonymous, he cannot be so in the preparatory "conversation of confession" (outside the confessional); he is appealed to by the penitent not only as a consecrated priest but also as a shepherd in his humanity and life-experience. He must, therefore, see clearly the relationship between the penitent and himself. The study of transference in psychotherapy shows, as through a microscope, what is happening: projections color the relationship in spiritual guidance too. If the priest now makes a mistake in his behavior, he receives more and more projections; he is seen and experienced not only as priest and father—which is legitimate—but as friend, brother, even lover. This causes a disturbance in the religious development of the future penitent. To strike the right attitude, to avoid becoming involved with projections as the therapist does, but to prevent them instead, is an essential part of the art of spiritual guidance. The study of the psychotherapeutic process requires insight, not only into the natural part of his pastoral relations in general but also into criteria for distinguishing between healthy and unhealthy relations.

(2) The alert priest does not consider it merely a matter of course that a man is ready to kneel before him in the confessional. This is such a great advance toward penance that the priest, moved by it, turns to him like a shepherd, or like a physician, and not only inquires after the sin but also, by seeing sin as a biographical item, considers how to help the other to disentangle himself, even if this is not immediately possible.

As a judge in the confessional, he must say what has to be done (according to the norms of moral theology); as a shepherd—and here his attitude resembles most that of the psychotherapist—he must also say how the other might *become* what he should be (this is pastoral care).

Therefore, he will not assume a negative attitude toward sin by hammering it home constantly, though he is clearly conscious of the sinful nature of an act. Just like the physician who does not fear contamination he will "hover nearby," because people often cannot extricate themselves from sin and the priest must not abandon them in their struggle. That means that he will try to establish some kind of relationship with them during their erring, even if it takes a long time. Only in this way can he appeal to them in the core of their person, which is the most important help, next to prayer, that he can give during the long time of development up to the step into the confessional, until everything has matured for this.

With this, exactly as in psychotherapy, the personality of the helper in the priest has come into a new focus. It is often the only point of contact for the relationship with God: the priest in his humanity is a medium for the word of the gospel which calls for penance.

6:   PASTORAL CARE
FOR SCRUPLES

I propose to treat this theme in two introductory remarks and two main parts from which we shall be able to draw some conclusions. The introductory remarks will show the scientific point of view as well as delimit the theme.

(1) Depth psychology has several fields of application: as psychotherapy in medicine; as "psychagogy" in education; and—extremely desirable—as "pastoral care" in pastoral theology. What new vistas of help are opened up to the pastor when he is acquainted with the findings of depth psychology! We are not going to talk about the way in which a pastor can exercise psychotherapy; but we are interested in determining his just position when confronted with a diseased soul.

(2) This should be explored with regard to the scrupulous, that is, with regard to those in whom exists that psychic pressure which manifests itself as fear of sin. Scruples are the manifestations of psychic sickness which the pastor encounters most frequently; man expects help from him. In these cases a very real, robust scrupulosity is pretended which is more or less valid for the whole spectrum of cases. How can the pastor, who is supposed to transmit supernatural strength, be of assistance? Should he be effective as a priest through the Sacrament of Penance, or is he called upon as a shepherd? The answer can be given in two parts: (a) he can do

so by treatment of symptoms, or (b) by treatment of causes.

I
TREATMENT OF SYMPTOMS

The pastor will first try to consider an analysis of different symptoms, wondering if this or that be mortal sin—and he will flounder right there. Scruples come from a different layer in the life of the soul than that claimed by the sacraments. Therefore, the scrupulous person does not belong in the confessional but in the reception room of the priest. Scrupulosity is a psychic ailment which has its own causes (and these will not be examined here), but which also brings into play a sphere of the soul that is necessary for the Sacrament of Penance, namely, the conscience.

Theodore Müncker defines conscience as "a function of the whole human personality."[1] Just as one organ of the body suffers from a malady which directly attacks another part, so conscience—as an organ of a sick psychic organism—is infected and cannot listen like an ear to the "personally engaging requests of the ethical 'you must.' " In other words, man no longer hears God's desires but the voices from the dwelling of his own soul; and a diseased conscience is no longer able to distinguish and judge a situation, its fault, and its position before God. This means that the scrupulous cannot sin; he does not stand before God as a sinner but as a sick man; and the priest cannot help through the grace of absolution but only with medicine for the soul. If a pastor wants to help the scrupulous person, like a shepherd,

---

[1] Theodore Müncker, *Psychologische Grundlagen der katholischen Sittenlehre* (Düsseldorf, 1953), p. 30.

he will not only bear with him, but even bear him—like a sick lamb; this means that he will temporarily relieve him of the responsibility for his sick conscience and take over its role himself.

There are now two in the reception room, the scrupulous one and the pastor. The scrupulous one arrives with a long history of sickness and reports about his years of suffering, his experiences with pastors—broad- and narrow-minded as he expresses himself—and about being upset when a confessor has taken seriously his confession of sins. He is a scrupulous person whose discretion cannot be relied upon at all. To succeed in obtaining an insight, it is important to let the ill one talk himself out. The pastor, listening quietly to him in this first encounter, will find out that:

(1) he has strong religious ties, and that his inner guide line is religious;

(2) that it would be the greatest disaster for him to be separated from God;

(3) that his own judgment about his stand before God is in cold contrast to his true striving; this discrepancy is the expression of a diseased conscience and thus he is being torn in two by excessive need for security, on the one hand, and by utmost insecurity about his rejection or acceptance on the part of God.

After this first session his past is not discussed any more, and he is advised not to mull it over. All his former confessions will be included in this "confession"; they were valid.

Which spheres is the pastor now to touch upon, when the scrupulous person's conscience is diseased? What part in the other is he to appeal to and to challenge? Not conscience, certainly, not even by reasoning. Only action is of help, that is, obedience. He is forbidden to confess. Very often the first involuntary reaction of the scrupulous is a deep sigh of relief, as if a great burden were lifted from him, which, however, is followed by anxious questions, uncertainty and shrinking back into unbelief.

The other person in the room, the pastor, slowly edges into the foreground of this initial skirmish; he still tries to offer a helpful position by arousing a recognition of sickness in his visitor. This may be done through comparing the house of the soul with its many rooms and stories and the throne hall in which he himself, the core of his person, is enthroned. In the basement, however, a gremlin has found access—no matter whence it came (it could be innate, that is, inherited, or acquired)—and it intends to roam all over the house of the soul and terrify its inhabitants—the will, reason, sentiment and conscience—making them insecure and frightened. Sometimes the gremlin kindles a fire in the basement and covers it with ginger root so that the smoke is drawn through all the rooms and poisons the atmosphere, until everything appears regrettable, bad, and sinful. Nobody knows if the gremlin can be removed through "surgery"; first of all, the sick man will have to take notice of his gremlin. "Until now you have been duped by him because you thought he was a judgment of your conscience; but your conscience cannot judge, because it is diseased. You have to make the decision if in the future you want to go on believing him, or if you will believe me, who tells you that you are not a sinner, that you cannot even sin and need not confess because you are sick and, in fact, must not confess. Confession for you is poison, not a medicine. What appears as sin to you is a gremlin, a sickness, something that is called psychic sickness, neurosis. Would you believe him or me?"

The scrupulous person's whole reaction, be it confiding or distrusting, can be summed up in the question: "Can you take on such responsibility? Do you really understand anything about it—as I feel you can and hope you do—but do not dare to assume?"

As a consequence, the pastor has to show his credentials, that is, prove his preparation—the study of this specialty, the books he has read and which can be shown (but not permitted to be read).

In addition to these outward credentials, he must be able to show the inner one—the assurance which permits him to take over religious responsibility. This can come only if he has been serious about the study of depth psychology—which understands the picture of the soul enlarged by the unconscious—and if he knows about the effect of the unconscious and about psychic sickness. This assurance springs from the fact that he himself has become existential—depending on the wholeness of his own nature—and that he is working on his own individuation.

This fact alone builds a bridge on which the scrupulous one can put his trust and confidence. For now he must decide if he is going to return. If he does so, it must be done on condition of "blind and complete obedience, which does not permit any deviation or by-pass," as Theodore Müncker writes. Thus obedience must be determined by acceptance of two definite vetoes: (1) no confession; (2) no turning to another priest with the same questions while he is coming to the pastor. If the visitor returns, it should be considered a sign that he has taken upon himself this obedience.

As the priest injects himself into the center of action, he takes over the direction of a soul in a situation which, more than almost any other case, requires and justifies obedience. The outward attachment through obedience, however, causes a vehement inner attachment on the part of the patient which by necessity focuses upon the priest the various images of archetypes in the patient: the shepherd, the physician or "medicine man," the healer or even Savior, the overpowering master, the Father; this means that the pastor is forced into this role by the patient and the atmosphere between them is charged with these influences. At the same time this also means that the pastor, with his entire personality, may be a passageway to God, insofar as he can solve the projected psychologisms. More about this later.

First, the conversations revolve about the examination of a "mirror of life." This should not be done by means of the commandments, as is the practice, but merely by mentioning the headings of the commandments. They are discussed as arrangements for the different phases of the Christian life without actually touching upon specific difficulties. This is an attempt to dissolve the fixation upon one commandment, for instance the sixth, and to show in a positive light the meaning of the commandments, the wishes of God, and His will. Many small scruples are dissolved by discussing Christian ethics simply because false information, faulty teaching, preaching with one-sided accents on some doctrines, and sickness have prevented the healthy development of human nature. Such one-sided interpretations of everything heard sometimes encase human nature so tightly it can no longer breathe.

But severe scruples are not reached by this means. One has to be careful not to raise new possibilities for sinning. For this reason the conversation about Christian ethics has to be conducted in a Socratic way; the priest will have to probe the anxieties and interpret or correct them, but he must never press for completeness and must not inject anything new. In the same way he will avoid touching upon the points of the scruples; it is only the general meaning of the Christian order of life which is to be discussed.

The result of these conversations will be to place a veto on the examination of conscience. Particular and weekly examinations of conscience, which the patient practiced before confession, must be omitted because in his case they are no longer a means toward improving the spiritual life, but rather a poison to the very disposition toward a spiritual life, a poison to the health of the soul. The objection which may be raised, that this procedure of no examination of conscience and no confession will cripple a man spiritually, has no foundation and can be raised only by those who have no insight into this sickness and are in ignorance of the further steps in treatment.

The next step is a conversation about sin, and should be undertaken in a twofold manner:

First, juridically. The trinity of serious matter, full recognition, and free will is necessary for sin. He who is sick in his soul, as is the scrupulous person, is hindered in his knowledge as well as in his free decision. This means, even in difficult cases, that no mortal sin is possible. Under certain circumstances the pastor must even write down the sentence, "You cannot commit a mortal sin," for reassurance. In any case it would be indicated for him to read aloud to the patient passages of Theodore Müncker's *Moral Psychology,* to point out to him that the book carries an imprimatur, and to underline the importance of this theological work. "In practice, the confessor will give the patient as a guide line the knowledge that no moral sin is possible with him" (p. 225). One might even have to go further and add: "Not even venial sin, as far as the Sixth Commandment is concerned." Objection must be raised against any hint that this may be construed as license. One may cite the psychiatrist Oswald Bumke, who states that "until now no case has been reported in which psychic pressures have triggered criminal action."[2] Nor has the author ever noticed a case where the decreased fear of sin in an overscrupulous person has brought with it licentiousness.

Secondly, what sin means must also be discussed on a different level, the personal one. Let us cite an example. When we grieve a wife or a friend, we know immediately how to repair it. But when a breach of trust takes place, such as adultery in marriage, the relationship is shattered. In the same way there are weaknesses and a breach of trust in the relationship with God—so-called venial sins and mortal sins. The religious life of the scrupulous person, so far, shows a religious guide line, and moreover this cannot be broken—it is what haunts his thoughts because the scrupulous conscience is sick; hence no breach of confidence with God, no mortal sin, is possible.

---

[2] Oswald Bumke, *Lehrbuch der Geisteskrankheiten* (Munich, 1942), p. 280.

The results achieved thus far will have to serve as ever-to-be-repeated content for further conversations: (1) no confession; (2) recognition of sickness; (3) obedience; (4) no examination of conscience; (5) no mortal sin. This repetition works like medicine, like tablets which are constantly being prescribed.

Thus, in the course of time, a platform is constructed on which the patient tries to walk; this means that more time may now be allowed to elapse between conferences—a week or a fortnight. The admonition in the end always must be: "Whom do you believe, the gremlin, or me? How did you feel before and how do you feel now?" Everything that has happened so far amounts to "crutches for the soul" or a guide on how to treat gremlins.

When occasion presents itself, advice can now be given which will have a general effect on health, such as a change in diet or increased use of air and water. Such advice must be chosen because its content has never aroused fear before, and it must be stated expressly that no sin is connected with it. It will be helpful to discuss such things in a witty and light-hearted way. Favorable as the effect of good-natured admonishing and scolding on the part of the pastor is for the scrupulous person, the pastor will still have to speak in a lighter vein when it comes to natural things, such as, for instance, converting a vegetable-juice drinker to wine-drinking, or feeding a carnivorous man with salads, or making it clear to him that some pious people do not want to swim because they feel too much "in God's hands."

Now, religious activity is slowly beginning to be regulated: There is a temporary freeing from prayer or services, even on Sundays, and from communion; a slow leading up to prayer,[3] starting with the daily sign of the cross; a participation in divine services in complete freedom; a partaking of Holy Communion in which the duality of communion piety will have to be underlined—the Sacred Host as spiritual nourishment, and the personal encounter with Christ—and a *sort* of confession (in general form, without examination of conscience and at predetermined times, such as every Easter or two to four times a year), on which occasion the "prohibitions," as discussed, and the "laws" would be mentioned. It is possible that the confessor will have to "carry" an overscrupulous person for many years, even for a lifetime. In one case, a discussion about "prohibitions" was scheduled for once a year only (during Lent) and followed by a general confession: "I confess that I have sinned in words, thoughts and deeds. I beg the Lord's forgiveness." That was sufficient for the whole year. It freed the way for communion every Sunday and for a life free from the sick fear of sin.

The question of healing arises continually: this the pastor cannot decide. But he can do what is necessary for both cases.

If no remedy is possible and the gremlin does not disappear, or cannot be cut out by "surgery," the time has arrived to speak of "the suffering as a cross of psychic sickness." This will be possible only if at least the distinction between Ego and sickness, between

---

[3] Fitting prayers can be found in the book by Chrysostomus Schulte, *Was der Seelsorger von nervoesen Seelenleiden wissen muss* (Paderborn, 1936), pp. 166ff.

Ego and gremlin, has been accomplished successfully. Sometimes such attitude of discernment and endurance is, in any case, to be sought because it will mean a crutch for the process of healing too.

Everything for which we have striven so far has as end the creation of an atmosphere, a space—a space for healing—in which some of the light neuroses may decrease by themselves, or in which a psychotherapist may work in case the patient should be referred to a therapist for diagnosis and future treatment.

Very often, outside conditions force the decision to refer the patient to a therapist: if there is a minimum of intelligence in him; if any therapist is available; if the financial part can be regulated, possibly by some kind of agreement (the psychotherapist's charity is often heavily drawn upon!); and if it is possible to entrust a psychotherapist with a religiously sick person such as the scrupulous.

Psychotherapy makes various demands and requests on the pastors. We are endeavoring to show how the pastor can work hand in hand with the psychotherapist; on the other hand, the pastor too has some very definite expectations of the psychotherapist who will treat one of his charges. It is desirable that the psychotherapist be a believer in Christ; that he is conversant with philosophical and anthropological questions; that he can discern the "difference of the Christian" and especially the differentiation between any kind of "natural religion" and Christianity. He should know all this, not only in theory but existentially, that is, that his search for individuation includes his being a Christian. Only thus will an understanding and a working together, hand-in-hand, be possible with pastors whose own search for individuation includes all layers of their own humanity.

II

TREATMENT OF CAUSES

If therapy is initiated the pastor has to lend a helping hand by holding on to the "healing space," thus helping the psychotherapist ("the patient cannot commit any sin") even if pent-up nature suddenly releases itself during therapy, for instance in a show of aggression against the parents which actually pushes the patient into real fear of the unconscious. Here again, as in the example of dispensation from one's Sunday obligation, the pastor may fall under suspicion of covering up for things which are not compatible with Christian ethics.

The best part of wisdom would be to keep silent. But this is not always possible on the part of the patient or another observer, and the priest is often exposed to the danger of calumny and denigration of character without being able to defend himself since he cannot betray matters of conscience.

Some priests, therefore, are rather reticent because of unhappy experiences; they might endanger other spheres of pastoral care by "going to bat" for one single person. Conversely, many a pastor has had to pay for dedication to one person with consequences harmful to himself. The one who knows supports this, knowing that "several levels of consciousness" are colliding with one another in our time.

But if no therapy is indicated for human or medical reasons, the scrupulous person remains a cross for the pastor. What can he do now which would reach beyond the treatment of symptoms as mentioned, beyond the "space for healing"—without exercising depth psychology? Even beyond psychotherapy, on the purely pastoral level there is a broad field of assistance remaining open which parallels psychotherapeutic action if it is approached in the right way of depth psychology.

To use a comparison, it is a problem of strengthening the other inhabitants of the house of the soul until the one who sits on the throne is again able to reign. He who sits there is often a small, frightened child—even in adults—who must mature into a responsible person. What is needed is pastoral care which has the character of personal challenge.

This is basically accomplished in four steps: the finding of the Ego (separation from the man-world and distinction of public opinion); the I-Thou relationship which means that the sexual and love life has to find its right place); the I-We relation (rightful insertion into the community; how pastoral conversation can help here in the course of years); and the I-God relation. We shall talk about this last at the end.

It is my experience that most scrupulous persons have never had a genuine encounter with God; they have talked in prayers; they have even touched Him in the sacrament; but what the gospel leads to, "Who sees me, sees my Father," has never happened to them. And yet the greatest strengthening of a person, the greatest challenge to our human person, springs from the fact that it is being confronted with the person of God—and as Ernst Michel puts it, it "is

to a definitive and personal existence."[4]
called forth from the general and typical 'being here'

This begins with the first instruction for confession, when the child for the first time officially meets the complex of sin, and where it is valid to say that a child cannot commit a mortal sin. (How often has this statement helped to relieve the scrupulous!) This endeavor is continued in the instruction for First Communion during which the image of God is influenced by the light or dark personality of the teacher of religion. All religious teaching might be the good tidings of the kingdom of God. It is good to be able to point to a Catholic catechism,[5] in which the whole ethics is presented as science of values and not of sin, without any false moral overtones. This would be continued further in the encounter of the adult with the gospel, for instance:

In the Sermon on the Mount the translation usually reads: "Do not be anxious for your life." But it means, "I forbid you to be anxious."

This is no harmless message from a Father-God who has pledged Himself to the welfare of His children on earth. Rather, we have to see what happens when worry is abandoned and the Christians do as the birds do. They can be found frozen in the snow. Man comes to the border and stops before an abyss into which he is pushed by death, into the dark, the gaping void, the Nothing, the deadly. And here the *faithful* finds a hand which catches him.

God has promised that those who serve Him will

---

[4] Ernst Michel, *Rettung und Erneuerung personalen Lebens* (Frankfurt, 1951), p. 68.
[5] *The Living Faith* (New York, Herder and Herder).

never be lost. Therefore, this anxiety about life, which is at the core of all worry, should be left to God! Thus, the anguish about the everyday concerns of life will change and will become lighter and not so compulsive, borne by some inner strength—the strength of faith. If this notion is developed in conversation, or in group work, or in a good sermon, it will nourish the soul by strengthening its core and permitting it to desire God. Thus the soul will—at least in some moments—be linked to the present. Psychic compulsion causes man to live either in the past or in the future. It is the transforming power of the gospel, when well preached, which makes man "present" again.

To cite another example: a business is based on the exchange of "I give and you give." The Pharisee wants to have justice based on his religious activity—in the same way many scrupulous persons do. But is God that way? One cannot even accounts with God, and there is no claim which permits us to compound security as we compound interest in our business ledgers. There can only be confidence in God's regard, in exchange for which He makes us the present of His love. This is something which must be brought home to the scrupulous person over and over again.

Then there is the conversation about the Son of God, who behaves so differently from what the archetypes suggest, such as the "pious" archetype with respect to the law forbidding the plucking of corn on the Sabbath (Mark 2:16); or the *King* who says, "My kingdom does not belong to this world" (John 18:36); or He who behaves differently towards sinners than towards the just (Mark 2:16)—He does not use His healing power according to their expectations (Mark 1:17); there is also the contrast of the *Son of God* and the *Ecce homo* (John 19:5). Christ is in complete contrast to the archetypes.[6]

When this is treated subsequently in the liturgical year, it influences the unconscious disposition in man. The preacher talks to the unconscious of his listeners and separates the Christ-image from the archetypes; he orders it so that the "appearance of God in the world" is put into focus, seen as it really is and not hidden by projections of the smeared Savior-image of the unconscious.[7] This is not psychotherapy or psychology in the gospel, but insemination of the gospel into human reality.

We have talked repeatedly about the role of the pastor in this encounter of man and God, between the scrupulous and God, between psyche and gospel. In the scrupulous person's promise of obedience to the pastor, this role is especially marked. The situation is parallel to therapeutic communication, except that the transference to the pastor happens in the spiritual sphere. "Need and *priestly* help" is, at least partly, of a different nature than "need and *psychotherapeutic* help." To speak in Jungian terms, the projected archetypes are differently accentuated and spring from a basic layer in which is contained the numinous. Equal in the two situations is the fact that the pastor is the model on which the patient practices (just as with the psychotherapist), and if the pastor acts true to himself (that is, as he is condi-

---

[6] In this context compare Goldbrunner, *Cure of Mind, Cure of Soul* (Notre Dame, 1963).

[7] Cf. Leopold Ziegler, *Überlieferung* (Munich, 1949).

tioned by his priestly, circumscribed way of life, by his true relation to the other as a brother or a sister, by his care as shepherd, and by his fatherly fondness for his child), the archetypes drop away from him. He is a model on which the scrupulous person practices his religious relations; and in his role as a priestly man, he is transparent to God Himself, who will heal all sickness in His kingdom.